BATTLES HASSLES TANTRUMS &TEARS

Good Housekeeping
Parent Guide

BATTLES HASSLES TANTRUMS &TEARS

*Coping with conflict and
creating a peaceful home*

SUSAN BEEKMAN & JEANNE HOLMES

*Hearst Books
New York*

Library of Congress Cataloging-in Publication Data
Beekman, Susan.
Battles, hassles, tantrums & tears: strategies for coping with conflict
and making peace at home / Susan Beekman and Jeanne Holmes.
p. cm.
Includes bibliographical references.
ISBN: 1-58816-038-6 (formerly 0-688-11937-9)
1. Parenting. 2. Conflict management. I. Holmes, Jeanne.
II. Title.
HQ755.8.B44 1993
649'.1--dc20   92-37608
CIP

First Paperback Edition 2001

1 2 3 4 5 6 7 8 9 10

Book design by Lisa Stokes
Cover design by Remo Cosentino
Cover photo © by Ron Chapple
Permission from FPG International

www.goodhousekeeping.com

Printed in the United States of America

To our families . . .

. . . the ones we were raised in, who gave us the roots that nourish us still

. . . the ones we live in, who continue to teach us what it means to create a peaceable family and a peaceable world

About This Book

ANYONE WHO HAS RAISED A CHILD—AND I'VE DONE IT TWICE—KNOWS that the experience can be delightful, amusing, inspiring, and—honestly—at times, frustrating. With this book, *Good Housekeeping* continues its tradition of helping mothers and fathers become better parents by offering clear and useful advice based on the latest thinking on the subject.

Written by two respected parenting authorities, *Battles, Hassles, Tantrums & Tears* provides terrific ideas and strategies that can help you bring up a child without bringing down the house. You'll probably find the anecdotes described in the book strikingly familiar; they've been taken from real-life parenting situations.

I hope that when you finish reading the book, you'll come away with a better understanding of your kids—and yourself. With luck, you'll also be able to reduce the number of battles, hassles, tantrums and tears so that you and your family can spend more time loving each other.

Ellen Levine
Editor in Chief
Good Housekeeping

Acknowledgments

THANKS TO SO MANY IN OUR COMMUNITY OF PARENTS, FRIENDS, AND family:

• Our Kamikaze Associates: William J. Kreidler, for his deep understanding of conflict resolution, his enthusiasm and encouragement, and for the title of the book; and Barbara Porro, conflict specialist extraordinaire and our number-one collaborator, beginning with hatching the big picture one hot afternoon on the deck. We'll probably still be working together well into the next century, refining the process as elders in rocking chairs.

• William Ury and Roger Fisher, for making conflict resolution accessible to real people.

• The dedicated parent educators in this country, to whom we are everlastingly grateful for inspiration and concrete strategies, including Barbara Coloroso, Elizabeth Crary, Stephen Glenn, Jean Illsley Clarke, John Taylor, and the Cline-Fay Institute.

• For reading, advice, and help framing and reframing our vision: Mary and Dave Bucy, Anna Chase, Cyril Gable, Jan Evans, Cathy Harlan, Sarah Lillie, Judith Kieff, Al Krug, Nondice McFall, Diana Mortlock, Linda Patterson, Barb Popoff, Kathy and Larry Riegel-Beek, Mary Lou Russ, Carol Young, Marijke von Roojen, Cliff and Cheri Pereira, Barbara Reuben, Gail Sadalla, Mary Jane Tonge, Dee Wendel, and innumerable friends in the Corvallis 509J School District for listening and for sharing their stories with us.

• For putting us up (or putting up with us) for the weekend or longer: Ruth and John Bregar, Susan and Clyde Curley, Kathy and Barry Kaditz, Naomi Krantz and Victor Dallons, and the Rarick family for sharing their cabin in the woods so we could get away from our families long enough to think about them.

• Toni Sciarra, editor par excellence, for keeping the big picture and the little one in her mind at the same time, and our agent, Eileen Fallon, for believing in us and giving us that little extra push.

• Claudette Hastie-Baehrs, Susan's therapist, for her common sense and grounding and for helping Sue update her inner and outer parent.

• Maryanne Dengler, for helping birth our work, and Susan Bliss, who had the wisdom to stand back and let our sparks fly, offering support when we needed it, and the rest of our "extended family," Shoobedebop, for nurturing us and being there.

• Our parents, Joanne and Wallace Heisner and John and Anna Marie Holmes, for their love and for all they taught us by being the parents they were.

• Our partners, George Beekman, our computer guru, for general availability and (especially) for bringing whole sections of the book back to life from the disk graveyard; and John Swanson, for his understanding of the gestalt, for freely sharing his professional expertise on parenting partnerships, and for walking his talk.

• Our children, Ben and Johanna Beekman, and Andy and Anna Marie Holmes-Swanson, for *all* the opportunities to try out our ideas, for the great stories, and for staying out of our hair so we could write it all down.

• And to the hundreds of parents in our classes and workshops, who willingly surrendered their public parenting images for the support of everyone else in lifeboats much like theirs.

Contents

Part One: Getting Comfortable with Conflict

Part Two: Using C.H.O.I.C.E.S. to Resolve Conflicts

Part Three: From Conflict to Cooperation: Building a Caring Climate

A Letter to Our Readers

DEAR READERS,

On an outing with our kids one day we huddled together on a park bench, lost in a conversation that rambled through topics ranging from newsy tidbits to classroom anecdotes. We were in the thick of a discussion about our mutual commitment to working for world peace when a disagreement between our six- and seven-year-old sons over a soccer ball escalated into a fistfight. We pulled them apart, picked each other up, and laughed at the irony of the situation. Apparently our kids weren't absorbing our peaceful ideals by osmosis!

Even though we were educators with over thirty years' collective experience in teaching kids from preschool to college ages, we were baffled. We knew we'd need some workable techniques for including our families in our plans for peace.

We began to share our daily frustrations as parents in more detail: hectic and unhappy mornings trying to get kids out of bed and to school on time, tense dinnertime dynamics, frequent struggles at bedtime, battles between kids. We'd both consciously chosen parenthood and worked hard to arrange our lives accordingly. This included reducing our incomes and scaling back our lifestyles when we gave birth to our first children. Despite our experience as teachers and on-the-job training as parents, however, we were often still at a loss as to how to handle daily conflicts. In place of the peaceful, loving family relationships we once expected would be ours, we found ourselves enmeshed in daily struggles. Much of our energy was spent smoothing ruffled feelings and facilitating positive communication. We were tired of the treadmill and tired of feeling responsible for putting out family grass fires, which seemed endless.

The two of us made a pact to support each other as we observed the effect of conflict in our daily lives. Soon we became aware of our personal tendencies to avoid conflict. We began to recognize how difficult it is to publicly acknowledge conflict in our lives, and how this had isolated us as parents.

We decided to survey the field of conflict resolution. We attended classes and summer workshops, conducted library research, and talked to experts in the field of conflict resolution.

Most conflict-resolution information has not been translated effectively for use by parents. The fields of family mediation and family counseling focus on families in crisis. We were looking for some help for the family that's basically healthy but wants to improve its ability to negotiate the choppy waters of little daily conflicts.

Gradually, by integrating conflict-resolution theory with specific parenting strategies, we were able to respond more effectively to conflicts with our kids. This gave us the confidence to rethink our old patterns of avoidance and to decide when it was appropriate to allow conflicts to emerge.

As we began to expand our options for dealing with conflict, we observed the benefits in our family dynamics. Positive management of conflict allowed family members to get feelings out and helped us understand each other better. We came up with creative solutions to problems that had previously seemed unsolvable.

As parents we were forced to become clearer about setting limits, defining for ourselves what was negotiable with the kids and what was not. We established clear family rules and routines for situations that had once been conflict-ridden. Our children's emotional expressiveness and creativity were developing new depth, tempered by empathy. They were also learning critical thinking skills and new options for dealing with conflicts in their own lives.

We were on to something. We weren't yet ready to apply as Families of the Year, but we were making progress. As we began to allow conflicts to emerge, we were forced to look directly at our own anger and to learn how to express it to each other and to our kids without being hurtful. We also needed to help our kids deal with their anger, which was no small task. Learning to resolve conflict as parents was turning out to be the most challenging and rewarding avenue for personal growth we'd ever explored.

While continuing to learn within our own families, we began to offer classes for other parents. Each class had similar dynamics: the collective sigh of relief as people shared their concerns, the hunger for new ideas, the shared excitement about breaking out of ruts and finding alternatives to "parenting by reflex."

In our classes, it became clear that no one solution was right for any family and that there were as many solutions as there were individual parenting personalities. Some folks found that the new strategies and support were enough to make a difference. Others found that they needed to significantly rearrange their lives to reduce the stress that was at the root of many of their family conflicts. One mother resigned from three committees; a father cut back on his hours at work. With each class we continued to discover the power to make creative change that is generated when parents get together to share frustrations and seek new solutions.

While we drew on a variety of parenting resources in our classes, none of them addressed conflict as directly as we had in our application of conflict-resolution theory. We began to develop materials for our own use, and soon it was time to put it all together and write a book.

We began to fit writing into our teaching and family schedules, spending after-school and whatever other hours we could steal at odd times. During most of our work our four children swirled around us. One of us tapped away at the computer while the other rode shotgun, serving snacks, taking carpool runs, negotiating kids' conflicts. The text and outline continued to form and re-form, based on feedback from our parenting classes, from our own kids and their friends, and from our students in our classrooms. We came to call it writing from the trenches, a military term that more accurately described our experience than any word in our peace-making vocabulary!

We've told all the stories and written the book in the collective *we*. We're all in this together: us, the parents in our classes, and all parents who are learning to create new responses to conflict in our lives. We invite you to join us in this learning community as we work together to find new pieces to the old parenting puzzles. Write to us and let us know what works for you. By sharing our stories and growing together, we can make peace begin at home.

How to Use This Book

BEFORE YOU TURN ANOTHER PAGE, BEWARE. YOU'RE IN DANGER OF overwhelming yourself with parenting ideas. Don't expect to put everything into practice right away. There's no quicker path to frustration, which has led more than one intrepid parent to give up completely on the idea of change.

In addition, beware of using this book to become more self-critical about all your little lapses as a parent. Take time to notice the skills you already have in place while you begin to pick up new ones.

Once you've read the book, we hope that you'll want to refer to it often and use it as a guide to changing your family's patterns for dealing with conflict. Knowing how busy all parents are, we planned most of the chapters to be read in one sitting. But we don't mean to imply that *reading* the information is the same as *applying* it with real families.

The most effective way to make parenting changes is to work very slowly on one aspect at a time, allowing at least a month to replace any outmoded patterns. Use your parental intuition about what changes you need to make. It's all part of a longer process, so focus on only one or two new ideas at a time. And celebrate success!

It may be helpful to find someone—your spouse or an accepting friend—to assist you in pacing yourself. We've found that sharing our experiences with each other gives us a new perspective. We're also less burdened if we don't feel responsible for making decisions alone, and we're likely to be more creative in devising strategies. Most of us exaggerate our own mistakes, and when we have a friend who can be accepting of them, we are better able to acknowledge them ourselves.

You might want to write in a journal as well as share with a friend. For some folks this is a great way to be reminded of goals and to stay focused on change. Use sticky notes as tabs to make relevant or useful sections accessible as you apply the ideas in your family in the months and years to come. The practice suggestions at the end of each chapter will also help you assimilate new information.

Conflict is handled variously in different societies in the world. Most of the basic principles in this book will work with a wide range of personal styles. We believe that they can be adapted to most cultures. Exploring conflicts stemming from different cultural assumptions and communication styles is essential when this is a factor within the family. Take what you can from our approach and use our recommended resources to guide you further.

Most important, take the time to honor yourself as a parent who cares. For every hour you spend helping your family resolve conflict, take half an hour to refuel and refresh yourself. The peace you create by this simple act will benefit your family as much as any other change you can make.

PART ONE

Getting Comfortable
with Conflict

"The problem is not that there are problems. The problem is expecting otherwise and thinking that having problems is a problem."

—*Theodore Rubin*

1
Beyond Anger and Avoidance

*"My kids physically taunt and torment each other. I
can't stand the hitting. I'm not even sure they're acting
out specific feelings; they just seem to hit just to hit."*
—Sally, parent of three

*"I wish I could get my son to do something without
screaming at him. He just sits there laughing at me, and
it drives me nuts. I'm about to pull my hair out over
this."*

—Carl, parent of one

*"I've read several books about sibling rivalry and
constructive discipline. I feel I'm gaining and applying
the techniques, but too many times I'm at a loss as to
how to handle daily conflicts and I revert to yelling and
threatening with punishment or hitting."*
—Anita, parent of two

SIBLING QUARRELS. UNCOOPERATIVE KIDS. FAMILY BATTLES. HOW ON
earth can a parent deal with all the everyday battles, hassles, tantrums, and tears that surface in the course of family life? We struggle to find ways to keep our kids from teasing and hitting each
other. We feel powerless to enlist our children's cooperation. Our
lives feel out of control. Self-help books counsel assertion and self-
awareness, but making these principles work in day-to-day family
life is difficult. Instead of the calm, patient, loving parents we want
to be, we are too often irritable, confused, and exhausted. Some-

times we lose our cool completely, scream at our kids, and feel guilty about it afterward. Sometimes we wonder how we got here.

When our children were very young, most parental advice centered on encouraging self-esteem. Many of us dutifully practiced the principles:

> Beth, a classroom teacher, had seen for herself the importance of self-esteem in facilitating learning, and she was determined that her children would have plenty of it. Her techniques were more than successful: When the family stopped at the park to take a break during a long car trip, two-year-old Christopher ran up to a swing set full of children, held up his hand like a police officer halting traffic, and yelled, "Stop, guys! Christopher here!"
>
> Christopher earned the name King Christopher. At times the title "king" seemed generous. Beth thought he was more like Attila the Hun, who may have been long on self-esteem, but who was distinctly lacking in empathy.

Like Beth, most of us have laudable ideals about raising our children. But when confronted by the reality of living with the children who possess the very qualities we've worked so hard to create, we have second thoughts. All the emphasis on creativity and individuality in children leads to frustration, as we try to balance adult power and kid power.

As we struggle to find this balance, conflicts abound. In addition we're caught in the inevitable crunches of career pressure and shifting gender roles. We lack the support of extended family and community. A scarcity of time collides with our own high expectations of ourselves as parents. The combined result of these stresses is a lifestyle packed with daily conflict.

CAN CONFLICT BE POSITIVE?

For many of us the word *conflict* is synonymous with unpleasant feelings, not getting what we want, a strained relationship, and sometimes verbal abuse or physical aggression. These associations may be so negative that we choose to avoid or deny conflict. The result of this denial is more conflict, which may produce more repressed feelings and lead to more explosions or pent-up anger.

This only reinforces our belief that conflicts should be avoided. So we spiral endlessly in the whirlpool caused by our inability to handle conflict effectively. We get little help from the society around us, because greeting conflict with denial, avoidance, or aggression is the cultural norm almost everywhere.

Some of us are so uncomfortable with conflict that we let our kids get away with murder, so to speak. We're relaxed, easygoing parents, who avoid unpleasant interactions with our children. We're the kind of parents who assume our children will naturally want to please us because we are so nice. But when we've had it, we are nice no more. We lose control and blow up, venting our anger by threatening, yelling, or hitting. This blowup usually obscures the issue that got us steamed up in the first place.

Others of us try to control our children's behavior in order to keep conflicts from emerging. We want to provide our children with firm guidance, and we expect them to respect our authority. We assume that our children will immediately respond to our direction. When they don't, we resort to threatening, yelling, or using physical force. Ironically we often end up in the same spot as our nonconfrontive counterparts who continually avoid conflicts.

Whether we greet conflict with avoidance, aggression, or both, we end up feeling impotent and stuck. Insecure about playing the parental role, we may try to avoid it altogether. Or we may try too hard and become overinvolved with our children, neglecting our own needs and creating dependency. Neither choice is healthy for us or our children.

Denial is so pervasive in our culture that sharing family conflicts with anyone but a spouse or close friend is taboo. This means that families are insulated from the social assistance that might help them resolve their conflicts. So the spiral of conflict denial goes on.

How to end the negative cycle of denial or aggression? Although most of us have a hard time believing that conflict can be positive, studies on family conflict show that the healthiest families allow enough conflict to reap the benefits of creative problem solving without allowing conflict to run rampant, which would disrupt family relationships. Other research shows that positive management of conflict helps nurture mentally healthy children. A recent study by psychiatrist Hans Steiner of Stanford University indicates that although many children and teens become compulsive about food sometime in their lives, those who become seriously ill share an inability to resolve conflicts.

Unfortunately few of us are naturally able to find this elusive balance between too much or too little conflict. That's where this book comes in. Through our work with parents and in our own families, we have discovered that family members *can* create solutions to problems that seemed previously unsolvable. Once we discover our own conflict-resolution styles, we have the perspective we need to become more capable of solving family problems. This is the first step in making peace at home.

MAKING PEACE ISN'T NECESSARILY PEACEFUL

When we think of a *peaceful* scene, most of us conjure up utopian fantasies. As a result we have unrealistic expectations about what a peaceful family should be. We envision a family in a perpetual state of peace and love. This romantic image must be replaced with an attainable goal if we are to feel successful as parents in the real world.

Let's replace our image of a peace*ful* family with one of a peacea*ble* family, a family that's *able* to make peace, a family involved in the ongoing process of resolving conflicts. Kids and grown-ups in a peaceable family are just like kids and grown-ups in any other family. The children haven't been injected with a serum that tranquilizes them into being nonviolent lambs for life. The parents are very capable of losing their patience, just like all parents everywhere. It is the process for dealing with inevitable conflicts that is unique.

The peaceable family is committed to forging its own unique set of conflict-management tools. Using our parental judgment, we experiment with new responses, learning what works in our own families. Each family's process is different, but the vision of a peaceable family contains these common principles:

- **Self-esteem.** According to Jean Illsley Clarke, an expert on children's self-esteem, this quality is nourished by recognizing one's own lovability and capability and by being recognized by others as being lovable and capable. Parents and children alike need to feel loved and competent. The entire family system works better when its members are secure in themselves. A child who has learned problem-solving and conflict-management skills will develop a sense of personal power, which will contribute to his developing sense of self-esteem.

- **Safe and respectful environment.** Children need to feel safe in the knowledge that there are clear limits for acceptable behavior. They need to feel that they will not be allowed to hurt themselves or others as they express their feelings and needs. Adults need to live in a home where they feel respected too. By setting limits for their children, parents create a climate that's safe and respectful for all family members. When conflict-management skills are taught in the home, children are more involved in the decision-making process. Although parents act as leaders of the team and must sometimes make decisions that are not negotiable, the needs of all family members are aired, and the environment that results is more respectful for everyone.

• **Caring and concern for others.** Empathy and caring for others is what Alfred Adler, a German psychologist who is highly esteemed for his work in child psychology, called social interest. This also includes an interest in making the world a better place. According to psychologist Jane Nelsen, "We have gone through an age of supermoms and superteachers where children have learned to expect the world to serve them rather than to be of service to the world. These are the children who think it is unfair if they don't get their own way. When others refuse to serve them they seek revenge in some hurtful or destructive way." To learn social interest, children must know how their behavior affects others. This learning needs to begin at home as children learn to express their own points of view and to listen to those of others. These are key elements of the conflict-management process.

• **Strategies for successfully resolving conflicts.** In Chapter 6 we outline options for responding to conflict. Each supports our goals of creating a safe and respectful environment where the self-esteem of parent and child are nurtured. Still, no two families look alike. Many times while writing this book we've uncovered terrific new strategies that worked perfectly in one of our families and bombed in the other's. As parents each of us understands best what will work in our particular situation. Likewise it's important to trust your own common sense as you try out the ideas in this book.

We make peace at home by changing habits, one by one. This may mean examining many aspects of our lives, from the way we deal with conflict, to the way we manage our time, to our choice of lifestyle. In the process the excitement and frustration of creating peace at home challenges us to grow as parents and as people.

Practicing

The following suggestions are intended for personal, partner, or group work. Choose those that will help you to deepen your own understanding or to integrate new ideas. Use writing or sketching as a vehicle for discovery or to explore your feelings and experiences. Let go of concerns about the final product. The questions that follow each activity will help you apply the concepts to your situation.

1. Using words or visual images, describe your idealized view of a family before you had children. How is this picture different from your family now? What problems do the differences between these images cause you?

2. Recall a time when you created something. Describe the experience, including your feelings about it. What positive associations can you bring to your new challenges as a creative parent?

2

How Do You Handle Conflict?

Papers rustled around the room as parents tallied their scores on the conflict-resolution-styles inventories. Some expressed surprise. Others discomfort. "I didn't realize I was an avoider. But when I think about it, I guess it is a pretty good description of my typical reaction to conflict at home." For this parent, taking the inventory marked the beginning of a series of changes in her parenting. She began watching her own pattern of avoiding conflicts in her everyday interactions with her ten-year-old daughter, and she made a commitment to change.

THE CONFLICT MANAGEMENT STYLES INVENTORY*

The conflict-resolution-styles inventory in this chapter is designed to help you identify how you *most often* respond when you have conflicts with your children. If you're like most parents, you've used every conceivable approach at one time or another. Think about how you reacted to the conflicts that have occurred in the past week or two. Choose the response that *best* reflects your typical reaction. There are no right or wrong answers. This questionnaire is simply a tool that has given many parents in our

---

*Adapted from a conflict-resolution inventory developed by William J. Kreidler in *Creative Conflict Resolution: More Than 200 Activities for Keeping Peace in the Classroom* (Scott Foresman, 1984). Used by permission.

workshops information about their natural tendencies in responding to conflict.

As you take the inventory, be careful not to make assumptions about the "best" style or to judge your own style. Each one is useful and effective in certain situations, and some children are nurtured by a stronger dose of one style than another. In addition, as children move through developmental stages, new approaches may be more appropriate. We'll consider the pros and cons of these styles later in the chapter.

Conflict Management Styles Inventory

DIRECTIONS

After reading each of the techniques listed below, decide whether you use it frequently, occasionally, or rarely. If it describes your frequent response, write "3" in the appropriate blank below. If it is an occasional response, write "2" in the appropriate blank. Select "1" if you rarely make the response described. Remember, there is no right or wrong score. Understanding where you are now gives you the opportunity to expand your choices.

When you and your child are in conflict, you usually . . .

1. Direct your child to comply with your expectations
2. Try to deal with your child's point of view as well as your own
3. Try to find a middle ground that is agreeable to both you and your child
4. Give unconditional support to your child's personality, creativity, and independence
5. Ignore your child's inappropriate behavior
6. Raise your voice and remain firm until your child complies
7. Find a solution that satisfies everyone's needs
8. Find a solution where each person gets something and gives up something
9. Let your child have his or her way
10. Distract your child by diverting attention or changing the subject
11. Keep telling your child to do something until he or she complies

12. Try to get all your concerns and feelings and those of your child out in the open
13. Give a little and encourage your child to do the same
14. Let go of your position because the issue is not worth the hassle, time, and energy
15. Kid or tease the child to deflect attention from the conflict

ANSWERS

I	II	III	IV	V
1. _____	2. _____	3. _____	4. _____	5. _____
6. _____	7. _____	8. _____	9. _____	10. _____
11. _____	12. _____	13. _____	14. _____	15. _____

TOTALS_____   _____   _____   _____   _____

SCORING

Add all the numbers in each column. The columns reflect five styles of resolving conflict. After compiling your scores, find which style or styles below correspond to your highest score.

I. **Directing:** Telling your child what to do; demanding that your child do what you think is right. For example, "Pick up your toys *now.*"

II. **Collaborating:** Working together with your child to explore the disagreement, generate alternatives, and find a solution that satisfies the concerns of both parties. For example, "It makes me angry that you left your toys all over the floor. Let's talk about this problem and find a solution that we can both be happy with."

III. **Compromising:** Finding a quick middle-ground solution that gives both you and your child part of what each of you wants. For example, "If you start picking up your toys now, I'll help you finish."

IV. **Accommodating:** Yielding to your child's point of view while choosing not to assert your own. For example, the parent may pick up the child's toys herself because the child is too tired to do so.

V. **Avoiding:** Not addressing the conflict, either by withdrawing from the situation, distracting attention from the conflict, or postponing the issue. For example, the tired parent might choose to leave the toys on the floor and deal with them later.

After you complete the inventory, decide if your score is an accurate reflection of your daily experience. You may find that two or more categories compete for top billing, or that you move back and forth between two styles. Does one feel more natural than the others? Sometimes our habits trick us into believing that what comes naturally works best. As we experiment with different approaches, the challenge is to increase our effectiveness by increasing our choices for dealing with our children.

As an avoider and an accommodator, Carol had difficulty taking a stand when immediate and decisive action was necessary. Carol was a single parent of two boys, ages six and eight. Because of her desire to encourage their creativity and self-esteem, **accommodation** and **avoidance** were her primary responses to conflict. This seemed to work well when the boys were younger, but as they got older, she began to resent the amount of work she was doing. She had little time to herself because she was always responding to her children's needs and requests. She also had difficulty taking a stand when immediate and decisive action was necessary. She found herself frequently screaming at the boys when they ignored her requests for help.

After becoming aware of her typical response patterns, Carol chose to expand her style to include **directing.** Our parenting class helped Carol target chores as an issue to work on with her children, and we helped her practice making directing statements and brainstorm what to do when the children didn't cooperate.

Carol explained to her sons that she felt she had been making some mistakes in the way she was handling things at home. She shared her frustration and resentment with them and said she was sorry that her bad feelings had caused her to lose her temper. She explained that she would be clearly stating her expectations in the future and described what would happen if they didn't respond. After they agreed on a weekly schedule of chores (**collaborating**), she announced that all jobs would be done before dinner (**directing**). When the boys finished their chores, the meal would be served. If they missed the regular mealtime, they could heat up the leftovers and clean up their own dishes. This was the case the first few days, but after a week the boys learned that Carol meant business, and mealtimes were once again fairly regular.

With a clear consequence in place, Carol was able to state her expectations calmly and let the consequence do the work of enforcement. She continued to develop her ability to be more directive with her children. As she gained confidence, she began exploring other strategies for resolving conflicts.

Dave was the parent of a bright and strong-willed seven-year-old. Even as a baby, Troy had a mind of his own. Dave was constantly getting caught in power struggles with Troy. He would order Troy to do something, and Troy would refuse. Dave tried everything he could think of: reasoning, yelling, punishing, time-out, withdrawal of privileges, logical consequences. Nothing seemed to work, and he was feeling powerless and ineffective as a parent.

In class Dave realized that his main conflict style was **directing.** This put him at loggerheads with Troy, who had a strong need to feel powerful. One area that was a consistent problem was Troy's unwillingness to get out of bed on time on school mornings. Deciding to try a **collaborative** approach, Dave took Troy out for pizza one night and shared his frustration about how things had been going in the morning. He asked Troy for help (**collaborating**). Together they came up with several ideas and then settled on a plan: Troy would get to have his own alarm clock, and Dave would remind him only once to get out of bed. If Troy made it to the breakfast table by seven-thirty, he could have his favorite breakfast: pancakes or frozen waffles. After that time he'd need to fix cold cereal for himself.

Troy and Dave found that problem solving helped them discover solutions that met both their needs. Troy liked feeling that he had some say in how he would be disciplined. An extra benefit: As Dave became less directive, Troy was more likely to cooperate on those occasions when an immediate directive response was necessary.

THE GOOD NEWS AND THE BAD NEWS ABOUT YOUR CONFLICT-RESOLUTION STYLE

Carol and Dave learned that their response patterns weren't necessarily wrong. They each noticed, though, that *using one style most of the time* led to trouble. Whatever your style, it has probably served you well some of the time. Each of these styles is effective in certain situations. It's the overuse of an approach that usually gets us in trouble. A parent who tends to direct her children may find herself embroiled in power struggles. An accommodating parent will probably soon discover that her kids tune her out much of the time.

Developing new strategies will add depth and breadth to your parenting. The next chapters are full of suggestions for expanding your repertoire. First, however, let's examine when each style is helpful and when it can get in the way.

DIRECTING

Directing is a useful style when immediate action is necessary or when you need to establish clear limits. If your seven-year-old is stalling around with toys after bedtime has come and gone, a firm command (followed up, if necessary, with an action or a consequence) sets the limit he needs. Directing is especially appropriate when safety is an issue. When your three-year-old wanders into the street and a car is coming, you want him to respond to your command *now*.

If directing is overused, some kids will tune you out. For other children a command may be like a call to battle, and you will find yourself locked in a power struggle. Others will comply, but will seek revenge or build hidden resentment. Overuse of directing can also intimidate children so that they are afraid to admit problems or give important information to their parents, fearing reprimand or punishment. As they grow older, they may choose to keep things to themselves or to rely on peers for advice and support. They may also come to lack initiative and look outside themselves for direction. In the teen years they'll be more likely to follow the lead of peers mindlessly, for better or for worse.

COLLABORATING

Collaborating, or problem solving, addresses the needs of everyone concerned and provides children with the opportunity to learn about another person's point of view. Collaboration is especially effective with a child who gets into frequent power struggles with his parent, because having control is usually more important than the issue itself is. Since collaboration addresses the needs of the parent as well as the child, both are empowered by this style.

Collaboration is not appropriate when time is limited or when the people involved are upset, hungry, or tired. Because of the time it takes, this is probably not the best choice for minor decisions.

COMPROMISING

If all else fails and the goals of both parties seem unreachable, compromise can break the impasse. Compromise is useful when fast decisions are needed on minor disagreements. On a harried morning when the kids are fighting over who gets to sit in the front seat for the ride to school, the parent who is adept at the use of compromise will create a quick solution: One child can ride in the front seat on the way to school and the other on the way home.

One drawback of compromise is the possibility that no one will be pleased with the solution. Also, if compromise is overused as a quick fix, larger issues that need to be dealt with may be overlooked. For example, constant sibling bickering about sitting in the front seat might indicate a need for more one-on-one parental attention. Moving from compromise toward collaboration might be an important next step for seeking a long-term solution.

ACCOMMODATING

Accommodating is appropriate when you recognize that you are wrong or when achieving harmony is the highest priority. You may also choose to accommodate when one issue is more important than another. When your child has not previously shown much interest in writing and is now working on scrawling out the letters in her name for the first time, accommodating her by letting her bedtime slide a little may be appropriate.

Too much accommodating may make a parent appear weak or wishy-washy, and it may overshadow the need for appropriate limits. The budding little writer may discover that pulling out the paper and pencil at bedtime is a good way to get to stay up later. In this instance the child may really need a clear message that it's time for bed, or she may need your help in devising a calming bedtime routine.

AVOIDING

Avoiding is a useful approach for minor conflicts that may be annoying but that are unlikely to result in a major negative outcome. For instance, bickering siblings on a long car trip might be distracted from their squabbling by a parent bursting into lively song.

Sometimes it's in everyone's best interest to avoid the conflict altogether: when you're in a hurry to get to work, when you or your kids are hungry and exhausted, or when you or the kids are too upset to think straight. You may also consciously choose to avoid a confrontation if you need time to think and prepare, or if confronting would be dangerous or damaging. If, for example, your anger at the child is too hot to handle, wait until you've cooled off. You can come back to the problem later, when you're feeling calmer.

As with accommodation and compromise, the denial of real problems that need to be addressed is the major pitfall of avoidance. For instance, distraction (a form of avoidance) isn't the best strategy for bickering car travelers who are in need of a rest stop, a food break, or more activities to do in the car. At worst, avoidance prevents parents from asserting their own needs or keeps them from establishing clear limits for their children.

Use the following chart for easy reference to help you appreciate the strengths and recognize the weaknesses of your dominant style or styles.

Pros and Cons of Parenting Styles

I.   **Directing** (telling your child what to do)
     Pros: Effective when immediate action is needed or when a child needs a clear limit.

Cons: Children won't learn to make decisions for themselves; they may also keep mistakes or problems from you, fearing a controlling reaction.

II. **Collaborating** (working with your child to explore the disagreement, to generate alternatives, and to find a solution that satisfies the concerns of all parties)
Pros: Helpful when you need a decision that addresses the concerns of everyone; teaches kids problem solving, empathy, and to predict consequences of their choices.
Cons: Too time-consuming for minor decisions or when you're in a hurry.

III. **Compromising** (seeking a middle ground by finding a solution that partially satisfies both you and your child)
Pros: Useful when all else fails; for fast decision making on minor disagreements, or when your goals are mutually exclusive.
Cons: Risk of not dealing with underlying problems; possibly not pleasing anyone; may be used to avoid setting clear limits.

IV. **Accommodating** (yielding to your child's point of view; paying attention to his or her point of view while choosing not to assert your own)
Pros: Useful when you see that you are wrong, when you want harmony, or when one issue is more important than another, such as when a child's telling the truth is more important than responding to the crime.
Cons: Ongoing problems may never be addressed. May be a way to avoid setting limits.

V. **Avoiding** (not addressing the conflict at all, either by ignoring the situation or by distracting attention from the conflict)
Pros: Defers confrontation on a difficult or painful issue until a more appropriate time; buys time to make a plan for handling the conflict; useful when the conflict is minor and no major negative consequences would result from avoiding
Cons: Issues may never get addressed; gets in the way of setting necessary limits.

The first step in making peace at home is to acknowledge the inevitability of conflict in family life. When we overcome our own denial and begin to understand our natural impulses, we become more skilled at maneuvering through the choppy waters of daily living, building our repertoire of strategies for shooting the inescapable rapids of everyday life.

Practicing

1. Recall a specific incident from your childhood showing a typical pattern of response to conflict in your family of origin. Describe it in words or images that communicate your family's general attitude toward conflict as you were growing up. Do you find the pattern from your childhood emerging during times of stress, or do you go too far in the opposite direction to avoid your family's pattern?

2. Is there one person in your current family who is most likely to be the peacemaker when conflicts arise? Which conflict-resolution style does this represent? How does that person feel about this role?

3. Remember an incident when you felt good about how you handled a conflict at home. What happened, and what made it work? Is there an element or strategy that could be applied to other situations?

4. What positive and negative reactions did you have to the descriptions of the conflict-management styles? What makes one seem more positive than another to you?

5. Think of a time when you tried a new parenting strategy and it didn't work. What went wrong? How can you apply this understanding to future situations?

3

Losing It or Using It: Managing Anger

WE CANNOT BE EFFECTIVE AS PARENTS WHEN OUR ANGER HAS OVERCOME our ability to reason. It's at times like these that we are most likely to yell, blame, threaten, or use physical force. These are the times we make decisions by the seat of our pants, reverting to tactics we swore we'd never use with our children. We make split-second emotional decisions we often later regret: "You're grounded for a month!" Sometimes we see the humor later. (One parent told her bickering offspring never to touch each other again for the rest of their lives. She became aware of the comic implications of this injunction when she shared her story in our parenting class.)

HOW IS A PARENT LIKE A RADIATOR?

Most of us deny anger. But anger, like a warm radiator, can give us valuable information about our needs and the fuel to get those needs met by making a change in our situation. If we ignore the signals, we lose the chance to address the problem that created the feeling in the first place. We also keep ourselves from learning to manage this complex emotion. Failure to acknowledge and address anger can be every bit as crippling to a family as an overheated radiator is to a car.

A CAR'S COOLING SYSTEM SIMPLIFIED

Several elements must work together in order for a car's cooling system to function well. Water recycles from the radiator through the engine, where it heats up and goes back to the radiator, where the fan belt cools it off again. Antifreeze in the radiator helps to cool the water while keeping it from freezing.

The temperature gauge on the instrument panel is an essential component of a car's cooling system. But the element that perhaps has the most impact on the system is the driver. If she is alert to the cues she receives from the gauge, she will quickly notice changes in the engine's temperature. If she isn't aware of how the system works, however, or if other demands distract her, the car may surprise her by boiling over.

When a car overheats, it's for one of several reasons. Poor maintenance may have left it with too little water or antifreeze or with a worn or poorly adjusted fan belt. The driver may have failed to notice the problem developing or ignored the gauge or other signs of trouble. She may have continued to push the car too fast or too hard in her eagerness to get to her destination. Some cars simply heat up faster than others and boil over more easily.

OUR ANGER COOLING SYSTEM

Our anger cooling system operates like the cooling system of a car. Like careful drivers tackling a mountain pass, we can keep an eye on our personal temperature gauge to keep anger within constructive bounds. This means being aware of how we are feeling moment by moment, tuning in to clues from our bodies or our behavior. For some people this might be tightening shoulder muscles, knots in the stomach, or a constricted feeling in the chest. For others emotional numbness or compulsive behavior (such as bingeing on food or anesthetizing ourselves with television) is the clearest early indicator of heating up.

Just as a driver can push a car too hard over the mountain pass, we sometimes push ourselves forward even though we're overstressed. During these times (and they are occasionally unavoidable) our energy and emotional reserves are drained, and we lose our tempers quickly and with little provocation. We may neglect personal maintenance, such as sleep and nutrition. We "overheat" quickly, without noticing the warning signs.

When we feel ourselves quickly heating up with our children, it is helpful to ask, *What is the real reason behind my anger?* It may have been a bad day at work, or we may have had an argument with our spouse. Although we may still need to deal with our children's behavior, it's only fair to check for other causes of upset before we pin it all on the children. If we discover a pattern of erupting anger, we may need to seek counseling to uncover the feelings or hidden difficulties prompting the anger. Or we may need to ask ourselves whether our lives are too out of control to handle and prepare to make significant changes.

We can't expect to rid ourselves of this strong emotion. In fact anger has many positive uses. It can propel us into action when something needs to be done, and it can bring to the surface feelings that need to be aired. We can learn to rechannel anger so that it's a productive force in our lives instead of a destructive one. But first we need to learn how to read our temperature gauge so that we can attune ourselves to our feelings.

LEARNING TO READ YOUR TEMPERATURE GAUGE

Learning to read our own personal temperature gauge is the key to channeling anger successfully, before it reaches the boiling-over point. Since many of us feel guilty about our anger, we're often out of touch with the early signs of trouble. Learning to read your personal temperature gauge begins with observing yourself as you move through the process of getting angry.

Connecting Your Anger Gauge: A Quick Quiz

What feelings do you generally experience before getting angry? (frustration, anxiety, fear, inadequacy, sadness . . .)

What thoughts precede the anger? ("I'll never get this right." "There's not enough of me to go around." "They never listen to me.")

How does the anger express itself in your body? (gritted teeth, tight shoulders, clenched hands, stiff neck, upset stomach . . .)

Does any compulsive behavior accompany it? (bingeing on food, alcohol, television, shopping . . .)

What situations are most likely to precede or accompany your anger? (whining kids in traffic jams, rushing to make it someplace on time, getting kids ready for bed . . .)

Despite numerous discussions about anger in our parenting classes, we still have trouble with our own temperature gauges. One Thanksgiving Susan was getting ready for company, and she had a million things to do. As she usually does when she is really rushed, she turned her automatic-pilot switch on and doubled her speed. The kids were supposed to be doing their chores, but when she went down the hall, she saw them playing video games. Unfortunately her unsuspecting husband happened on the scene at that sensitive moment and caught the full measure of Susan's fury when he asked if she'd seen his missing keys. For Susan the first step of reconnecting the temperature gauge was to begin to notice her shoulders getting tight, one of the physical symptoms that usually accompany her anger.

Jeanne noticed herself compulsively searching for junk food one day after tangling with her willful son. She had told Andy that he needed to take a shower, and he had refused. She'd looked him square in the eye and informed him that he'd better be in the shower in the next five minutes or else. He had stomped up to his room and slammed the door. She had headed straight for the kitchen. It was only after she finished the whole bag of chips that Jeanne realized how furious she really was. If her temperature gauge had been hooked up, she could have saved herself a whole lot of unneeded calories.

Often parental anger disguises helplessness or fear of failure. Dan, a single parent of twin daughters, described a time when he was very angry with one of the girls. "I knew I was going to get hooked into her behavior. Even though I realized what was going to happen, I didn't know what to do about it. And then I really blew up." For Dan feelings of helplessness usually preceded explosions at his daughters. Other parents have expressed these thoughts: "Sometimes when I ask my kids to do something it's like I'm invisible. I don't exist. It makes me furious," or "I feel like I'm replaying stuff my mother did, which is something I swore I'd never do. But when I'm in a situation I don't know how to handle, I usually lose my temper."

The first step in managing your anger is to understand your anger cycle. Like the driver on a mountain pass, watching your temperature gauge will help you begin.

BREAKING THE ANGER CYCLE

Early research in the field of anger management advocated venting anger by freely expressing it. The theory was that humans, like volcanoes, need to expel their anger to get it out of their systems. Venting anger harmlessly can be helpful in some situations. For some people, however, expressing angry feelings actually *increases* the intensity of the emotion. It also won't solve the problem that led to the feelings.

When a radiator boils over, it's usually an indication of a bigger problem in the engine. Angry outbursts can serve the same function. First, we must see anger as an indication that something is wrong and needs to be changed. Second, we need to learn to communicate our needs caringly in order to work out a solution. Anger management helps us to use this powerful emotion rather than being at its mercy.

Preparing for anger can help us understand and deal with it constructively. We can keep ready-made strategies up our sleeves for staying cool and for cooling off. We can use what we know about ourselves and our families to create anger-defusing strategies that will work for us. Our plan should include knowledge of the four stages where intervention is most likely to succeed:

• Pre-anger

• Heating up

• Before boiling over

• After boiling over

PRE-ANGER

Pre-anger is the period before a conflict occurs, when the situation is ripe for anger to brew. Sometimes, by reading **environmental cues,** you can head off trouble before it gets going.

When he returned home from work, for example, Jeanne's husband, John, found that "sniffing out the scene" by checking for clutter and noticing how he was greeted was the best way to tell how Jeanne was coping with their new baby and their rambunctious preschooler. He had discovered that **gathering information before entering the scene** was the first step in giving his partner the support she needed at that time of day. Both Jeanne and John had learned that they needed a plan in place for John's reentry. This usually meant that he took over with the kids while she got dinner on the table. At other times Jeanne could read the tension in John's face and give him some unwinding time before joining the family. On days when they'd both had it, at least they knew what they were up against.

Certain **times of day** are fertile ground for eruptions. According to one researcher, seven times more family fights occur before dinner than after people have eaten. No wonder some family therapists call this time arsenic hour. Veteran parents also unanimously recognize the volatility of bedtimes and the time between getting up and leaving the house on weekday mornings. Knowing this can help us make better decisions about how to handle a potential conflict. For example, feeding a snack to a cranky child can go a long way toward heading off predinner battles.

Our **stress level** may be high from overcommitment, time crunches, lack of sleep, illness, or life in general. When you're feeling stressed, ask yourself what **feelings are below the surface.** Take a minute to relax, turn inward, and see if you can trace the source of your irritability. Volatile scenes at home can be touched off by frantic deadlines at work or by a misunderstanding with a friend. Sometimes figuring where the stress originated and letting the family know is enough to head off an eruption.

Jeanne recently received the news at work that the application for a large grant that funds her program had been denied because the application form had been lost. While preparing dinner that evening she stopped herself as she was about to bark at her kids for some trivial transgression. She realized that her irritability had less to do with her children's behavior than with her frustration about the situation at work. She took a moment to share with Andy and Anna Marie what had happened:

"You both need to know that something happened at work today that is bothering me and I'm feeling *very* irritable right now. I could easily blow up at you tonight. I need lots of hugs and your cooperation this evening."

Awareness of the problem doesn't make it go away, but at least it increases everyone's understanding. Jeanne and the kids kept the evening low-key, and the kids even tucked her in at bedtime.

A blowup also can be avoided by reducing the source of the stress or by giving yourself a break. Sometimes a quick mental mini-vacation (described on page 50) can give a needed shot in the arm.

HEATING UP

We begin to heat up when we become **emotionally engaged** in the conflict. Learning to read the signals indicating that we're being "hooked" emotionally by what is happening is invaluable in managing anger. Let's look at the breakfast battles at Brenda and Erik's house to illustrate how to manage anger at this stage:

> Of course it was on weekdays when everyone was trying to get out of the house on time that Brenda's and Erik's seven-year-old son, Jack, would whine about what was being served at breakfast. He ranted about how no one cared about what he liked, how his brother always got what he wanted, and how it wasn't fair. Brenda, an accommodator, wanted to avoid a scene at the breakfast table. She was also concerned that Jack start the day with good nutrition, so she tried to cajole him into eating. Although she was annoyed by his attitude, she was too busy trying to keep things moving to notice her feelings.
>
> Sometimes Brenda's efforts worked and sometimes they didn't. More often breakfast ended in a blowup with Jack, which left everyone in a rotten mood. Jack would often react with a temper tantrum and get revenge by not being ready to leave the house on time, making Brenda late for work.

It's useful to **notice when you're getting hooked.** If you don't acknowledge your anger, you run the risk of allowing it to smolder until it flares out of control. Brenda, for example, tried to be patient with Jack, suggested alternative foods, joked, tried distracting him and even ignoring him. But all the time she was accommodating him, her anger was building, and she didn't recognize it until after she'd blown up.

One morning Brenda felt herself getting hooked one more time and decided she'd had it. While the family finished breakfast, she retreated to her room and pulled out an anger checklist that she'd picked up in our parenting class:

• At what point am I getting hooked? (*The minute I hear him whining about breakfast.*)

• What is the origin of the anger? (*No matter what I do, I can't seem to please him.*)

• Is this anger an indication that I need to be doing something differently? (*Yes. I feel resentful and upset, and I don't want our day to start on such a sour note.*)

- Is immediate action necessary? (*No. I can let it go for this morning, but tonight I'm going to talk to Erik and make a plan for how to handle this in the future.*)

- Is further cooling off needed? (*Yes. I think I'll finish getting dressed before I go back to the breakfast table.*)

By getting some distance from the situation and asking these questions, Brenda had already taken the first step in managing her anger and using it to change the breakfast conflict.

Self-talk is an effective strategy at this stage of the anger cycle. You can use it to move yourself through a potentially explosive situation. The Family LifeSkills Program from the Palo Alto Medical Foundation describes four steps of self-talk useful in all stages of the anger cycle. Brenda might have engaged in self-talk this way:

- Preparing for potential conflict (pre-anger): *This breakfast could be difficult. Remember that what's important is keeping myself calmer in the morning. Don't get hooked by Jack's behavior. There is no need for an argument. I can handle this without blowing up.*

- In the conflict situation (pre-anger and heating up): *As long as I keep my cool, I'm in control of the situation. Think about what I need to do. Stay focused, and don't blame Jack or call him names. Remember not to yell at him.*

- In the middle of the conflict (getting hooked and heating up): *My stomach is starting to knot up. Detach and count to ten. My anger is a signal that something needs to be done. Jack may be trying to hook me into being angry, but I'm going to deal with it constructively. I can solve the problem later.*

- After the conflict:

If the conflict is not resolved: *I'm letting go of this for now. Thinking about it only makes me more upset. I will make a plan with Erik when I'm feeling better. It's time to relax and cool off. It's probably not as serious as it seems right now.*

If the conflict is resolved: *I did a great job handling that breakfast situation. I'm getting better at dealing with my anger.*

Try **expressing your anger to your child.** Putting your anger into words can help disperse it. Remember, your child needs to know how his behavior affects others. It's important to avoid blaming and name-calling, which usually escalate the conflict and, if used frequently, can be damaging to your child's self-esteem.

A "feeling statement" (discussed further in Chapter 10) is a very effective tool for expressing anger in a way that is respectful to others without diminishing the way you're feeling. In the situation above, Brenda might have said, "Jack, when you whine and complain about the breakfast, I get really annoyed and upset and I start my day in a crummy mood. I'd like breakfast to be a pleasant time for all of us." This feeling statement might have helped Brenda to manage her anger until she had time to cool down and work with Erik and the rest of the family to develop a plan for handling the stresses of weekday mornings.

If you feel yourself reaching the point of no return, **buy some time to cool down.** Sometimes just a few seconds will be enough. One parent found it effective to detach emotionally from the situation by thinking of a time when she felt very successful as a parent. Take a few slow breaths. Although it sounds like a cliché, counting to ten is another quick way to put a little water back in your personal radiator. Often listing the problem on a posted family meeting agenda, as suggested in Chapter 12, gives immediate relief. No matter what you do in those few seconds, the simple act of detaching and changing gears can derail a destructive outburst. Remember, it is okay to feel angry. But when it has reached the point that you are about to lose control of your behavior, it is time to pull over, cool off, and think about how you might act differently the next time you're in the situation.

BEFORE BOILING OVER

This stage refers to the few split seconds before you completely lose your temper. Even when you feel that an angry outburst is inevitable, you can still change the course of your anger. Feeling statements are effective here also. Some parents recommend messages such as "I'm about to lose my temper!" or "I have just *this* much patience left!" (Say it like you mean it!) Some families have a verbal or nonverbal signal (such as a time-out hand motion) that warns kids when the adult has just about reached his or her limit.

Self-talk, such as Brenda used to handle her anger at the breakfast table, is a powerful, quick approach you can use anywhere: *I can choose not to blow up. I'd better take a quick break before I really lose it.* If you have more time, treat yourself to something that renews you and helps you feel cared for. It's helpful to have some ideas in mind that you can easily remember when you're heated up. The following is a list of cooling-off strategies brainstormed by parents in one class:

• Take a bath

• Dig in the garden

• Bake a cake

• Smash the cans for recycling

• Retire to your room with a favorite book

• Take a fantasy trip in your mind to a tropical paradise

• Call a friend and vent

• Go for a walk

• Write in your journal about what happened

• Do housework

If you choose to remove yourself from the situation, state clearly to your child that you are too angry to talk and will come back and deal with the problem when you are feeling better. **Your child needs a clear message about how you're feeling and what you're going to do:** "I'm feeling really angry and I need to take a time out so I can cool off." When you do this, you are clarifying a situation that may be confusing or frightening to your child, and you are modeling for your child how to manage out-of-control anger. We'll talk in Chapter 11 about helping children deal with their own anger. For now, though, remember that how you handle your anger sends your child a very important message about how he might handle his.

AFTER BOILING OVER

Even the best of parents sometimes boil over and do or say things they later regret. The time after you boil over can be an opportunity to learn from your mistake and reconnect with your child. Before you try to move ahead, however, check to see if you are completely cooled off. If you aren't, use one of the cooling-off strategies that you know will work for you.

Jane Nelsen, author of *Positive Discipline,* suggests that you "share with your child what you didn't like about your behavior and ask for help for a better solution." She uses the *"Three Rs of Recovery"* to do this:

• Recognize: "Wow! I made a mistake."

• Reconcile: "I apologize."

• Resolve: "Let's work on a solution together."

Seventeen-year-old Jill and her boyfriend, Craig, took Jill's fourteen-year-old sister to a drive-in movie in the family car. They promised Carmen, the girls' mother, that they would be home after the first movie, at 10:30. From around 11:00 until their arrival home at 12:27, Carmen's reactions moved from concern through fear to panic. When the girls and Craig arrived at the door, she was there to greet them.

They had given a friend in need a ride home, they explained. Carmen's fear switched to rage as she asked in her most controlled voice why they hadn't called to tell her of their change in plans. When they said they "hadn't seen a phone," she lost it, cataloguing all the phones between their house and the drive-in. She stopped short of name-calling and asked Craig to leave. Then she and her daughters had a shouting match, and all three of them stomped and slammed their way to their rooms. After reading for a while Carmen had cooled off, but she was still unable to fall asleep and finally decided to get a glass of milk. Jill was in the kitchen doing the same thing. Carmen said, "Jill, I'm sorry I yelled at you in front of Craig. I know it's a mistake to lose my temper like that, and it embarrasses me when I do it."

"There's no way you could be as humiliated as I was in front of Craig tonight!" Jill snapped back. Carmen resisted the urge to get hooked by her daughter's angry response. She took a slow breath, reminded herself that she could handle this without blowing up, and simply stated her feelings about the situation.

"When I don't know where you are late at night, I get really worried about you and I imagine all the bad things that might have happened to you. After I see that you're okay, I just feel angry for having wasted my time and energy on worrying. What can we do so that this won't happen again?"

Jill suggested that Carmen could just stay in her room and keep her mouth shut, for starters. Carmen (after quickly reminding herself to stay calm) agreed that she'd like to be less involved in the girls' lives, but said she could do that only if she were sure about their safety. She proposed they talk the next day about ways to solve the problem. Brainstorming ideas later, when both of them had cooled off, they compromised: Jill agreed to call if she knew she'd be more than half an hour late. Carmen said that from now on she'd wait until they had privacy to discuss upsetting issues.

Once she'd cooled off, Carmen used feeling statements to communicate her needs. Problem solving was also a useful tool for arriving at a solution that was comfortable for both mother and daughter. A big bonus was the valuable model Carmen gave Jill of an adult who could admit mistakes and learn from them.

Be gentle on yourself when you make mistakes. You will lose your temper sometimes. See this as an opportunity to learn how to use your anger for constructive change. Know that you will have another chance to do it differently next time, and begin preparing.

MAKING A PLAN

Often you can identify situations in which conflicts regularly occur. Rehearsing for anger can help you stop the anger cycle and deal constructively with the conflict. Having specific ideas for handling a situation and knowing what you will do if your child doesn't cooperate can help reduce the feelings of helplessness that may be fueling your anger.

Erik and Brenda, whom we left earlier in the middle of breakfast battles, recognized that they needed to change how breakfast was handled. Later in the week they called the family together, and the children were informed that breakfasts were going to be different in the future. Whining and complaining were not going to be allowed at the breakfast table. If someone didn't like what was being served for breakfast, he could go fix some cold cereal. If the whining continued, the complainer would be asked to leave the table or would be removed from the table if necessary. Jack was informed that his mother would be leaving the house at seven forty-five. If he was ready to leave, he was welcome to have a ride. If not, he could walk to school on his own. (Since he hated to walk, they knew this would be an effective consequence for him.)

With some nutritional guidance by Brenda, Jack planned the breakfast menus for the week. Involving him in this part of the process helped give him some power in resolving the problem. While breakfast was not always without discord, Brenda and Erik both found that they lost their tempers much less often after they had a clear plan of action. They no longer felt as if they were at the mercy of Jack's whining and tantrums at the breakfast table.

To create your own plan of action, ask yourself the following questions and rehearse new responses mentally:

• When might this situation occur?

• What will I do?

• How might my child react?

• How will I respond to my child's reaction?

• What are my options if my child does not cooperate?

• If I am getting too angry to deal with the situation constructively, what are my options for cooling off and for dealing with the immediate situation with the kids? (Imagine yourself taking these steps in detail, including two or three possible outcomes.)

TIME AND STRESS

Time and stress often play a major role in the anger cycle. Sometimes you need to put your feet up and take a look at your life. It may be time to reevaluate your priorities and decrease your time commitments to reduce the tension in your daily activities. Brenda found that getting up fifteen minutes earlier took the rush out of getting ready and helped her relax and be less irritable with her son on workday mornings.

When her kids were young, Susan was constantly stressed from running late all day. She decided to make some changes. She became aware that she tried to do too much in the amount of time available to her. As she planned her day, she tried to be more realistic about what she could get done. She consciously decided not to do the "one more thing" that was making her late before she left the house. She discovered that she was able to be much more patient with her children when she wasn't operating on a hectic schedule all day long.

Sometimes recurring anger calls us to look deeply at our way of life. Coping with schedule hassles, child-care crises, and staying centered as a couple and as a family require enormous emotional resources. Some couples make a conscious decision to reduce their consumption of luxuries and services in order to buy more time for their families. In some cases this means moving to a different location in order to avoid a long commute, or taking less demanding jobs. Although for some families this is a financial impossibility, if stress-induced anger is disrupting your family, it may be worth contemplating.

Sometimes anger is an indication of a deeper difficulty. Deep-seated anger that stems from childhood abuse or that causes us to mistreat our children emotionally or physically usually requires outside help. If we find ourselves frequently losing control and unable to change the pattern, we owe it to ourselves and to our children to seek professional guidance.

Practicing

1. Post the chart "Anger: A Guide to Keeping Cool" (at the end of this chapter) someplace where it is easily seen, such as on your refrigerator or bulletin board. Target the stage of anger that's most difficult for you to manage. Try some of the ideas. Share the results in a journal or with a friend.

2. Brainstorm a list of cooling-off strategies that work for you. Be sure to include some ideas that can be implemented in a few seconds. To get started, ask yourself what you like to do to nurture yourself.

3. Try taking a five-minute minivacation as a cooling-off strategy when you're feeling stressed: Find a comfortable position to sit in or lie down and take a few deep breaths. Think of a serene place you have visited in the past: the mountains, the seashore, a hammock in your backyard. Put yourself into your mental scene and imagine all the sights, sounds, and smells. Experience the peacefulness and notice your body relaxing. Stay in this calm state for several minutes. Enjoy the serenity. Slowly bring yourself back, knowing you can retain the relaxed feeling, even though you may be faced with difficult situations. You can return to your special place whenever you wish.

Anger: A Guide to Keeping Your Cool

PRE-ANGER

Stress check:

Tune into body signs of stress.
Check for compulsive behaviors or thoughts.
Take a minivacation, mentally or physically.

Feelings check:

Am I angry about an unresolved situation with another person?
Am I angry about an unresolved problem with this person?
How can I plan to act on these feelings next time, in order to avoid bringing them with me to this new situation?

Time issues:

Am I rushed to keep a commitment or schedule?
Is this a dangerous time of day for conflict in my family? (early morning, predinner, bedtime)
When you're relaxed (with partner, friend, at a family meeting), prepare for how you will handle tense times.

Environmental clues:

Look for physical evidence of stress (clenched jaw, tight shoulders, knot in the stomach).
Use this evidence to plan your response creatively.

HEATING UP

Acknowledge your anger:

What is the source of my anger?
Will the anger fuel a constructive or destructive action?
Is immediate action necessary? (safety issues)
Is further cooling off necessary?

Self-talk:

I can handle this. I know what to do.
I can keep my cool. I don't need to get angry in order to regain my control over the kids.
I don't need to make more out of this than it's worth.
They may be trying to hook me into being angry, but I'm going to deal with it constructively.

Express anger to your child:

Avoid blaming, name-calling.
Use feeling statements: "I feel angry when _____ because _____."

Use Cooling-off Strategies:

Count to ten.
Put problem on family meeting agenda.
Other cooling-off ideas that work for you . . .

BEFORE BOILING OVER

Use feeling statements: "I feel irritated when the kitchen is left messy from afternoon snacks because it's hard for me to cook dinner."

Tell your child, "I'm about to lose my temper!" or "I have just this much patience left!"

Use cooling-off strategies that work for you. If you need to remove yourself from the situation, be sure to tell your child why you are leaving and that you will return and deal with the problem when you are feeling better.

AFTER BOILING OVER

Take time to cool off.
Use the Three *R*s of Recovery:

Recognize—"Wow! I made a mistake."
Reconcile—"I apologize."
Resolve—"Let's work on a solution together."

Let go of your mistakes!

AFTER THE ANGER CYCLE

Plan what you will do next time:

Have cooling-off strategies up your sleeve.
Practice self-talk.
Rehearse what you will say and do.

Problem-solve for recurring situations:

When might this situation occur?
What will I do?
How might my child react?
How will I respond to my child's reaction?
What are my options if my child does not cooperate?
If I am getting too angry to deal with the situation constructively, what are my options?

Use family meetings or discussions with your partner or friend to problem-solve.

4

Overcoming Self-defeating Messages

"Because I had to follow so many rules as a child, I wanted my daughter to be raised differently. I gave her lots of freedom in order to encourage her independence and creativity. As the years went by, however, I found myself becoming angry with her demanding attitude. I began to see that indulging her with freedom was draining my time and energy, and I felt resentful. It wasn't until she got older and began to have difficulty following directions at school that I realized we really had a problem."

—Eileen, parent of two

"I'm constantly battling with my teenage daughter over everything, from dress to curfew. I'm so afraid she's going to be wild like my sister was and mess up her life. Even though she hasn't gotten into any trouble, I still worry about what will happen if I don't keep her in line. I just don't want to lose control."

—Bruce, parent of one

THOSE OF US WHO ARE **ACCOMMODATORS** AND **AVOIDERS** ARE AMBIVA-lent about disciplining our children. We get tripped up in our own confusion about what limits are appropriate. Nevertheless, settling conflicts within the family is one of our primary opportunities to provide the structure children need to make sense of the world and to experience the consequences of their behavior.

Those among us who are **directors** obstruct effective discipline by reacting too quickly, controlling our children's activities and behavior when we need to lay off and help our kids learn to set their own limits. We may also forget to listen to their point of view. Combining discipline with good communication helps children develop the empathy they need to become sensitive, caring adults.

This is why we owe it to our kids to claim the power of effective discipline. However, in the pivotal moment when we need to respond to a child's unacceptable behavior, fleeting thoughts that prevent us from taking effective action may lurk just below the surface:

Maybe I didn't say clearly enough what I wanted.
If I bend on this one, I'll lose my authority.
Oh, she's had a hard day.
If I'm strict, my kids won't like me.
I don't want to make a scene in front of the relatives.
I'm starting to sound like my dad, and I don't want to be that way.
He's just not old enough to understand.

These self-defeating messages may reflect our needs to be liked, to change our own childhood, to be fair, to be sympathetic and supportive, or to feel in control. Ironically many of these negative thoughts come from our positive desire to be conscientious parents. Although they may have their origin in our ideals, just as often they stem from our fears.

• **Fear of damaging the child's self-esteem, independence, or creativity.** The emphasis many of us place on nurturing these qualities in our children leaves us timid about setting limits that might impinge on the development of these precious traits. Some parents resent living in the chaos created by children's art projects, yet they don't want to interfere with the creative process by asking kids to clean up the mess. The mistaken thought might be, "If I make them clean up this mess, it might discourage them from even starting a creative project next time."

As these children grow older, many become demanding and inconsiderate of the needs of other family members. We find them more and more difficult to live with. We are raising powerful children, but at what cost to ourselves? And what lessons are our children learning in the process?

• **Fear of conflict.** Many of us have difficulty setting limits because we want to avoid conflict with our children. By whining,
crying, arguing, or throwing temper tantrums, they teach us to
expect such a negative response that we find it easiest to avoid
dealing directly with the behavior. When we protect ourselves from
their outbursts, however, we are protecting them from learning to
manage their own anger or disappointment.

The biggest cost of this response is that the temper tantrums and
manipulation generally escalate. We end up having to endure more
of the negativity we originally tried to avoid. We're often caught in
this dilemma in public places, where we derail ourselves by thinking, "I'll just let her have what she wants this time. I don't want
to be embarrassed by a scene in front of all these people." The
child quickly learns that this kind of public behavior pays off.
Sometimes the behavior becomes so obnoxious that you end up
taking drastic action you later regret. Either way you learn plenty
about the heavy cost of avoidance.

• **Fear of our own anger.** Many of us were raised with a strong
message to control our angry feelings, so as adults we're still uncomfortable about experiencing this emotion. Others have painful
childhood memories of parental anger. Still others have been
frightened by the power of their anger when it has erupted vio-
lently. As we come to understand our anger patterns, plan ahead
for tense situations, and learn to trust our ability to communicate
anger appropriately, we can overcome our fear of this strong emotion and use it as fuel for positive change.

• **Reaction to authoritarian upbringing.** "Fear," "isolation,"
"a shrinking feeling"—parents describe these childhood memories
when they recall conflicts in their family of origin. Many of us are
determined to avoid the authoritarian parenting approach that we
associate with these memories. Thus those of us from authoritarian
families may not hear the inner voice that says, *I've had enough.*
Because we never learned to know and stand up for our rights as
children, it is difficult for us to do so as adults. Instead of dealing
directly with unacceptable behavior, we replay our habitual responses, ranging from endless patience to placating to nagging.
When we've finally had enough, we vent our anger at our kids
directly by yelling, blaming, or hitting, or indirectly by withdrawing
or using sarcasm.

An authoritarian upbringing may also cause us to give privileges or freedom to our children that we wish we had been allowed. A parent who regrets not being allowed to play dress-up as a child might have difficulty defining what clothes are permitted for dressing up until her daughter stains Mom's favorite skirt when she wears it to a pretend tea party. The self-defeating thought that kept this mother from protecting her clothes might be, *I wish my mother hadn't been so picky about letting me wear her clothes.*

The hazard of becoming antiauthoritarian is that we may easily overlook the child's real needs for structure and clear messages about the effects of her behavior. Overpermissiveness neglects our family members' right to an environment that is physically and emotionally safe and respectful. Parents need to feel respected, just as children do, and if kids are in charge, we forfeit that right.

• **Fear of the disapproval of others.** Sometimes the worst enemy of limit setting is our interest in preserving our image with our kids, their friends, or other adults. We've all experienced the discomfort of needing to discipline our children when we have guests in our home. Many children use this to their benefit, consciously or unconsciously. Removing your child to a private place to deal with the problem is one good strategy in this situation.

When a public confrontation occurs, some parents are afraid to allow consequences to occur naturally for fear of appearing uncaring in the eyes of other adults. Ease these awkward situations by explaining what you're doing to those around you. One parent we know got tired of nagging her dawdling kindergartener to get ready for school. She knew that his favorite time of the school day was at the beginning, when he played with classroom pets, so she decided to stop nagging and allow her child to be late. She dealt with her concern about being seen as an irresponsible parent by sharing the plan with her child's teacher. After her son discovered what he missed when he was late, he began to move faster in the mornings.

• **The need to be in control.** In trying to avoid feeling ambivalent and helpless, some parents rush to direct, command, or rescue their children. These parents may want to protect their children from being hurt by the inevitable mistakes kids will make. By not allowing children some power to make their own decisions and to learn from their mistakes, we rob them of opportunities to learn responsibility. A parent who stands at the door every day with her child's schoolbag and lunch removes the chance for her child to learn to organize his things. She may defeat herself by her caring: *He's got so much on his mind. If he forgets his bag, he might get a bad grade.* It may help to ask yourself whose problem you're solving before you get involved.

Sometimes we defeat ourselves by having unrealistic expectations about how our children should be. It's this image that is behind much of our discipline. Even the most caring parents become overcontrolling when they try to fit a real child into an idealized image that may or may not suit that child. It's important to have *realistic* goals for our children. But we need to look carefully at the strategies we use to move toward those goals. If we're overcontrolling, our children may become rebellious and sneaky. Conversely they may lack initiative and become too dependent on others for direction. This may lead them to be overly vulnerable to peer influence in their teen years.

USING SELF-TALK TO CONQUER SELF-DEFEATING MESSAGES

If you're an avoider or an accommodator and have difficulty setting limits or acting decisively when your child behaves inappropriately, self-talk may be helpful in countering your critical inner voice.

For example, when you know you need to follow through, yet you find yourself faltering, stop. Ask yourself, *What am I saying to myself that's keeping me stuck?* When you hear yourself think, *Gee, maybe I didn't say it clearly enough,* you might say to yourself, *It may not have been perfect, but I know I stated what I expected them to do.* A parent who is strongly directing or authoritarian may be crippled by a different kind of self-defeating message: *If I give in, he'll think he can get whatever he wants in the future,* or *If I'm too permissive, she's going to become a drug addict like the kid down the street.* Again, we can respond with self-talk: *Showing a little flexibility on this minor issue doesn't mean I can't take a stand when I really need to.*

Early in the process of writing this book we were struggling with the first draft of the chapter on following through with discipline. Even though it was a sunny spring day (a rarity in Oregon), we were determined to stay put at the word processor to finish the chapter. Our daughters, Johanna, seven, and Anna Marie, five, had disappeared from the yard, even though we'd made it very clear that we expected them to stay within earshot of the house when they were playing outside. We'd been working on establishing house rules for our writing sessions, and the girls had both been pushing the limits.

Jeanne called for them, and we waited, listening for a response. After five or ten minutes we were anxious enough about the girls that we were having trouble concentrating. Frustrated, we decided to stop working and go out on a search. As we stepped out on the deck, both rosy-cheeked girls strolled around the corner, long wispy blond hair shining in the spring sun, each clutching a bouquet of wildflowers from the meadow behind the house. Johanna looked at us sweetly, holding out her fistful of flowers.

"These are for you, since you couldn't be outside today," she said.

We stared at each other in silence. We both knew what the other was thinking: *How could we discipline the girls for breaking a rule under these circumstances?* We accepted the flowers and thanked them, and then we held a quick conference as they went indoors for a drink of water.

"Speaking of following through on discipline, what are we going to do now?" Susan asked Jeanne.

"Well . . . uh . . . hmmm, I guess we do need to do something, don't we?" Jeanne answered.

"Okay. We know we need to have clear limits around here, or we won't be able to work, right?"

Even though we were disarmed by the girls' thoughtfulness, we decided that they needed to know that we were serious about the earshot rule. We sat them down for a little talk.

"We want you to know how much we loved and appreciated the flowers, *and* it's also important for you to remember the rule about staying within earshot. Since you had trouble remembering the rule today, you'll lose the privilege of leaving the yard for the rest of the day." After a few weak complaints they bounced out to play again.

Once the girls were outside, we asked each other what made it so difficult to follow through in this situation. Even though we knew what we *should* do, we thought about what it would mean to take a disciplinary stand at such a precious moment. We reassured ourselves that we could appreciate the girls' intentions and still apply limits and that we'd have more struggles in the long run if we didn't hold the line on the rules we were trying to establish. By working together we uncovered the self-defeating message in this scene and talked ourselves through it. Doing this made it easier to act decisively.

Take time to uncover the messages that keep you stuck. It helps to talk it through with a friend or your partner. Once you uncover the messages that are most incapacitating to you, you'll be able to create self-talk that is truly effective. The chart at the end of this chapter will help you recognize common self-defeating messages and give you ideas for self-talk scripts.

Sometimes just comparing your goals to the reality you've created is shocking enough to motivate a radical change from old patterns:

Debbie was a sympathetic and caring single parent. In the early years of parenting she poured much of her energy into making a creative and stimulating environment at home for her kids. When they were older, she gradually became aware of how much she'd waited on them in the early years. If she didn't pick up, the house became a jumble of kid clutter. One night when she was sick with the flu, she asked her twelve-year-old to heat up frozen dinners for the family. He reacted as if she were making a selfish and unreasonable request.

Lying in her bed that night, Debbie realized that she had taught her kids to expect her to be the housemaid. When she imagined what her son would be like as a roommate or husband if she let things continue as before, she cringed. This experience gave her the clarity she needed to provide the limits that would train her son to be more sensitive about how his behavior affected those around him. The next morning she posted a reminder to herself on the refrigerator: TODAY'S SON IS TOMORROW'S ROOMMATE.

This became Debbie's self-talk refrain as she worked toward setting limits relating to cleanup and household chores. She also learned to notice when she was beginning to feel taken for granted, and became able to clarify the limits she needed to establish in order to feel respected as a parent. Whenever Debbie started to waffle on this issue, she reminded herself of her goal by using her self-talk motto and calling up the image of

her son as an adult with his future spouse. This
motivated her to stay on target.

Most negative messages are created by our love of our children
and by our desire to be good parents. We become sidetracked, not
because we are lazy or incompetent but because we care so much.
If you find yourself consistently unable to reduce the power of
these debilitating messages, however, a parent-support group or
a counselor may help you uncover the issues that are immobiliz-
ing you.

As we begin to gain control over our inner messages, we meet a
new challenge: We need models of ways to follow through on
discipline, and we need to practice replacing old reactive patterns
with new choices. Otherwise we're apt to stay stuck. The next
chapter offers a rich assortment of strategies for follow-through
and practice in using it.

We don't need to be rigidly consistent in overcoming negative
messages. In some situations flexibility is the best policy. However,
listening too often to your inner critic will undermine your ability
to set limits effectively. To gain perspective, discuss your concerns
with a parenting partner, friend, or parenting group.

Practicing

1. Try noticing and jotting down self-defeating messages for a couple of days. Discuss them with your partner or a friend. What fears
are reflected in these messages? What is the source of this fear?

2. On a sheet of paper write your most frequent self-defeating
messages in one column. In a separate column list possible comebacks to argue with the critical voice. The next time you hear the
negative message, play the comeback in your head. Share what
happened with your partner or friend.

3. Think of a situation in which you're at a loss as to how to
respond. Imagine the self-talk you'll use to change your usual response. Envision how your kids will react and how you'll respond.
Try it out and report to a friend or parenting partner.

Common Self-defeating Messages and Positive Self-talk

If you have difficulty setting limits and following through, look over this list of self-defeating messages to see if any apply to you. We all use them appropriately at one time or another, but *if you are frequently derailed by them*, practice the self-talk responses suggested here, or make up your own.

SELF-DEFEATING MESSAGE	COMEBACK
I'm tired (or rushed), and dealing with this right now is the last thing I need.	*I can let them know I intend to follow up on this after I've rested (or when I have time). Or I'd better follow through anyway; it'll just get worse if I don't.*
I'm so angry now that I might say or do something hurtful.	*I can buy some time to cool off and then deal with this later, when I'm calmer.*
Maybe I didn't say clearly enough what I wanted.	*I may not have said it perfectly, but it was clear enough.*
I don't know what to do (or how to follow through). I might not do it right.	*I can buy time and think about it, check out resources, or brainstorm with a friend.*
If I bend on this one, I'll lose my authority.	*I'll be more effective if I'm flexible and try out other approaches.*

SELF-DEFEATING MESSAGE	COMEBACK
I don't want to make a scene in front of our guests (in-laws, relatives, etc.).	*It's more important for my child not to get the idea that it's okay for him to act this way in front of other people than it is for me to save face. I can take him back to my bedroom, where it's more private, and deal with it there.*
Oh, she's had a hard day.	*If I always let the rules slide when she's had a hard day, how will she learn to take responsibility for her behavior?*
If I discipline here (in a public place), he might make a scene, and it would be really embarrassing.	*If I don't deal with it now, the behavior will get worse, and every time we go into a store, we'll have a scene.*
If I'm strict, my kids won't like me.	*I really want them to like me, but it's also important that I not let them walk all over me.*
I'm starting to sound like my dad, and I don't want to be that way.	*I can think of another way to handle this situation. I'll buy time to think about it.*
He's just not old enough to be able to deal with this.	*He's old enough to do lots of things. I think he can handle this. In the meantime I'll check with other parents and see what they think.*

SELF-DEFEATING MESSAGE	COMEBACK
I can't be consistent about enforcing this, so I'll let it go.	*I don't have to be perfectly consistent in order to follow through effectively. I can figure out some way to handle this. It's too important to let go.*
What she's doing now is really not okay, but she's so cute.	*This behavior may be cute now, but if I let her continue, it won't be so cute when she gets older.*
I don't want to damage their self-esteem (or creativity).	*I want them to grow up to be responsible and respectful of others. Setting limits doesn't have to hurt their self-esteem (or creativity).*

5

Meaning What We Say:
Following Through

"My five-year-old, Clark, seems out of control. When I ask him to do something, he ignores me. No matter how many times I ask, he just keeps at whatever he's doing. Often I end up losing my temper with him. Even a whack on the bottom doesn't seem to do any good; a little while later we're at it again.

"Clark's mother and I divorced a year ago, and we have joint custody. I really wanted to make the time he was with me positive, so I gave him a lot of slack. I also felt guilty about how hard the divorce was on him. Now his behavior is getting to me. I guess I was defeating myself by feeling sorry for him and by thinking that he wouldn't want to be with me if I was too demanding. I think this self-talk stuff might make it easier for me to move on this, but now that things have gotten so out of hand, what do I do?"

—Bill, parent of one

OKAY. WE'VE LEARNED TO PUT OUR FOOT DOWN. NOW WE NEED TO know what to do once the foot is down and our kids don't seem to notice or care! Children quickly figure it out if we don't mean what we say, and they respond accordingly. Follow-through is the key, and we need several methods that will work for us in a variety of situations.

THREE APPROACHES TO FOLLOWING THROUGH

• **Take direct action.** Move people or objects. For example, lead your child *gently* by the arm over to the coat that needs to be picked up from the floor or to the dirty plate that needs to be carried to the kitchen. *This should be done matter-of-factly, before your anger tempts you to exert excessive force on your child.* If direct action is not working or if you are unable to do it respectfully, consider using consequences, described below.

• **Duties before privileges: "When you _____, then you can _____."** This approach pairs a responsibility with a privilege: "When you clean your room, then you can go out to play." Parents often ask how this is different from a bribe. When we use a bribe, the child is simply being rewarded or paid off in some way for acceptable behavior. With the "when you _____, then you _____" strategy, children are learning about the logical progression of taking care of responsibilities before playing. This strategy, like all follow-through strategies, must be stated calmly. When you say, "You can't go outside until your room is cleaned up" with a scowl on your face and hands on your hips, it becomes a threat.

Empathize with the child's feelings of disappointment or anger if he loses the privilege, but treat the decision matter-of-factly: "I can see you're really disappointed that you can't play this afternoon. Maybe you'll choose differently next time." This avoids moralizing or preaching, which is a temptation in these situations. It may be necessary to repeat this script many times. Don't be too concerned about boring the child with repetition. It will help to avoid power struggles if you avoid emotional displays, stay calm and loving, and remain matter-of-fact.

• **Use consequences: "Either you can _____, or _____will happen."** This strategy allows the child a choice between a desired behavior and a consequence: "Decide peaceably which TV show you two will watch, or the television goes off." Offering this choice is a way to deliver a command or a directing statement with some clout.

There are two kinds of consequences: natural and logical. A *natural consequence* allows nature to teach children what was wrong with their choices. The natural consequence for refusing to eat dinner, for example, is to be hungry later in the evening. Allowing children to experience the natural results of their choices without rushing to rescue them from the consequences of their decisions is sometimes difficult for parents. So long as the child is not harmed or endangered in any way, however, natural consequences can be an effective teaching tool. Children need to learn that their choices cause specific results that directly affect them.

For those inappropriate behaviors that have no natural consequences, we can use *logical consequences* to establish cause-and-effect connections for the child: "Since you took off on your bike without a helmet, you'll need to park the bike for the rest of the day." These consequences require planning and follow-through by the parents, but the choice whether or not to take the action and face the consequences can be posed to children.

CONSEQUENCES OR PUNISHMENT?

A *consequence* is directly related to the misdeed, and it gives a real-life lesson to children about what might happen when they behave in certain ways: for example, if you don't put your clothes in the laundry hamper, they don't get washed with the family laundry. The consequence is that your favorite outfits are not clean on Monday morning. On the other hand, a *punishment* might look like this: The child who forgets to put the laundry in the hamper receives a scolding and is sent to his room for failing to do what he was told. The lesson about what happens when you don't put your clothes in the laundry gets lost in the process.

Punishment, imposed by the parent, is designed to make children suffer for their misdeeds. Discipline and punishment were one and the same for most of us as children. Our parents assumed that we'd learned our lesson if we'd suffered sufficiently for our wrongdoing.

Many parents experience punishment as a way to regain power, which we feel we lose when our children behave inappropriately. Unfortunately in winning the battle we may have lost the war. Punishment is often humiliating to children, who may appear to cooperate but who will often reclaim their power through sneakiness or other subtle rebellion. In addition, feelings of anger or revenge often distract children from taking responsibility for their misdeeds. These same feelings may erupt in the teen years as open rebellion. Unfortunately by this age it's more difficult to gain cooperation if punishment has been the foundation of your discipline style.

An equally important concern is the question of what we are teaching our children when we use punishment. We're teaching them that might makes right. We're teaching them to heed the voice of outside authority, which may make them more vulnerable to peer pressure. We're teaching them to fear our retribution, which encourages them to sneak around behind our backs. We're teaching them to work for external rewards or for others' approval rather than from internal motivation, which may set them up to depend on material goods or substances to make them feel good. The real tragedy is that the fear, power, and revenge issues that surface around punishment may permanently damage our relationships with our children.

A consequence can easily become a punishment. The way you deliver it is important. Keep your tone calm and friendly and make a simple statement: "Since you went to your friend's house without letting me know where you were going, you will lose the privilege of leaving the yard for the rest of the day." If you add comments such as, "I've told you a thousand times not to do that," or *"This* should teach you a lesson," your child will experience the consequence as punishing.

CONSEQUENCES: PLAN AHEAD

Parents who are operating by the seat of the pants often end up applying their consequence to that part of their child's anatomy. Instead, when you see a behavior becoming a problem, anticipate the next time the behavior might occur and plan your strategy. Brainstorm with a friend or partner, or improvise from the consequence chart at the end of the chapter. Discuss the problem with your child and let him or her know ahead of time what the consequence will be. As you become comfortable with this follow-through strategy, involve your children in choosing the consequences.

For example, Jeanne's husband, John, was getting tired of reminding the kids to clear their plates from the table when they were finished eating. He brought the issue up at dinner one night. "I get frustrated when I always have to tell you to clear your plates after meals. Does anyone have any ideas for a consequence for this?"

"We could hire someone else to do the dishes," joked Andy.

"How about if we pay Dad a nickel if we forget to clear them and he has to do it for us?" Anna Marie suggested.

"Maybe we should have to wash them if we forget to clear them," Andy added.

"That sounds like something I'd be comfortable with," said John. "How about this: If you don't clear your plate by the time I finish the dishes, you will have to wash your own. Let's say you'll have to wash them before the next meal." Everyone agreed, and the plan went into effect immediately.

Sometimes a consequence is called for, even if the child has not been informed of it ahead of time. At age seven Jeanne's daughter, Anna Marie, helped herself to the family camera and shot most of a roll of film (she didn't even know how to focus the camera). Jeanne felt that it was important for Anna Marie to take responsibility for helping to pay for the costs.

"You know, it's not okay for you to use the camera without asking Dad or me first. It's very expensive to buy film and have it developed. As a consequence you will need to help pay for buying new film and getting this roll developed. Does three dollars seem like a fair amount for you to pay?"

"I guess so, but I don't have that much money right now," Anna Marie answered.

"How about if I make a list of some jobs for you to do to earn the money?" Jeanne suggested.

"Okay. And on the chalkboard in the basement I'll keep track of how much money I made," Anna Marie added.

During the next week Anna Marie did a few jobs each day to help pay for the cost of the film, and Jeanne and Anna Marie both felt satisfied with their agreement.

Some parents get stuck when trying to come up with a consequence on the spot. Fortunately you don't need to. You can always buy time to think of an effective consequence and talk to your child about it later. Let your child know that there will be a consequence, but that you want time to think about it first. Then retreat and discuss it later. As a bonus you're more likely to be calmer. You might decide to involve your child in selecting the consequence as part of your plan.

HINTS ON CHOOSING CONSEQUENCES

Parents who are new at implementing consequences are sometimes boggled when they try to start. The first question we usually hear in our classes is, "So how do you figure out a consequence?"

THE THREE R'S OF CONSEQUENCES

In her book *Positive Discipline* psychologist Jane Nelsen offers three practical guidelines for choosing a consequence, which she calls the Three *R*s. A well-chosen consequence, she writes, is *reasonable, respectful,* and *related.* A *reasonable* consequence is appropriate to the child's age, the degree of the crime, and is workable for the parent. It's probably unreasonable to expect a three-year-old to repaint a wall that she's decorated with marking pens, but it *is* reasonable to put the markers away for a few days. Grounding a child for six months as a consequence for coming home late from a date once would be punishing to the parent in addition to being out of proportion to the crime. *Respectful* consequences avoid humiliating, embarrassing, or excessively blaming the child. Forcing an older child who is a sloppy eater to move his place by the dog's dish is not respectful. A more respectful consequence would be to give the child a choice between improving his manners or eating alone after the rest of the family is finished. *Related* consequences are connected to the crime. The child who goes to visit a neighbor without telling her parent of her intentions loses the privilege of leaving the yard for the rest of the day.

CHOOSING CONSEQUENCES BY CATEGORY

In an article in the *Journal of Individual Psychology,* psychologist Jerrold Gilbert divided consequences into three categories, which may prove helpful to you in generating ideas.

• **Loss or delay of privileges:** Privileges lost or delayed include activities; interaction with others; use of objects; or access to areas of the house, yard, neighborhood, or other space related to the problem. Privileges can be delayed until the child has completed the desired task. For example, a child who repeatedly harasses another child in the company of a friend loses the privilege of association with that friend. Or a privilege is withdrawn temporarily because the child has demonstrated through his behavior that he is unable to handle it responsibly. For example, a child who ties up the phone for two hours might be restricted to five-minute phone calls for a period of time.

• **Loss or delay of cooperation:** Living in a family is a cooperative venture. Children may lose parental cooperation if they fail to fulfill some aspect of their responsibility. A parent who has spent extra time doing chores the child has neglected to do won't have time left to drive her son to his friend's house.

• **Compensation:** Compensation may involve repair or replacement of an object, or a time or work trade. One child who was in the habit of hanging from the rim of the backyard basketball hoop finally bent it and had to replace it as a consequence.

One of the handiest strategies is the time trade, which can be applied to a variety of situations. For example, when Jeanne's son, Andy, was nine, he didn't come home after school one day. Jeanne, beside herself with worry, called the homes of several of his friends. They hadn't seen him. She stuffed four-year-old Anna Marie in the backseat of the car and started cruising the streets searching for him. Even a stop at his school failed to turn him up. Finally she decided that the best strategy was to go home and wait by the phone. Surely he would call.

At five-thirty he came through the door, two-and-a-half hours late. Jeanne was fit to be tied. Andy explained that he hadn't thought about calling since he was so excited about the first day of practice.

Jeanne knew she was too upset to come up with a good consequence on the spot, so she bought time. She informed Andy that most of her afternoon had been spent looking for him and worrying whether he was okay. She let him know how angry and upset she was and that she and his dad would be talking to him that evening about a consequence for his late arrival. When Jeanne's husband, John, arrived home later, they discussed the situation and decided to offer Andy a choice of consequences. He could owe Jeanne two and a half hours of work time in trade for the time she had lost that afternoon, or he could lose the privilege of going out after school for a week. Later they talked to Andy, explaining how upsetting it was to Jeanne when he didn't come home at the usual time and she didn't know where he was. Andy chose to trade time for his consequence, and from then on he was much more conscientious about getting home on time.

Finding effective consequences takes time and practice. The chart at the end of the chapter lists common examples of consequences that other parents have implemented. These ideas may help you get started. As you get the hang of it, you'll discover the strategies that work best for you and your child, and you'll become more adept at improvising new ones.

If you just can't think of a consequence that is reasonable, respectful, and related, then switch to another follow-through strategy, such as direct action or "when you _____, then _____," or try problem solving (discussed in Chapter 10) with your child. A consequence easily becomes a punishment if you have to stretch too far to come up with it, and your child won't understand its connection to his unacceptable behavior.

It's important to remember that consequences aren't the only strategy for following through. Also, once you get the hang of consequences, it's easy to overuse them. Not too long ago Susan's fourteen-year-old son, Ben, didn't wipe off the kitchen counter after fixing himself some toast. Susan said, "Ben, I've been noticing that you're not cleaning up after yourself when you make snacks. We're going to have a consequence for that."

"Mom," Ben peered over his glasses at his mother. "Don't you think you're getting a little infatuated with consequences?"

He was right. Susan realized that she and her husband, George, had gotten into the habit of delivering consequences like ultimatums, and they were starting to feel like a punishment to Ben. It was time to reconsider. They decided to focus more on problem solving and on getting the kids involved in setting their own consequences. Remember, the important thing in the long run is not to maintain your parental authority at all costs but to develop workable solutions to problems.

TIPS FOR APPLYING CONSEQUENCES

- **Give your child a simple, direct statement** expressing your concern that she has chosen that behavior and the consequences that will follow. Express your confidence that she will choose another behavior next time: "It's too bad that you chose to _____. I'm sure you'll make a better choice next time."

- **If you are very upset or angry, take some cooling-off time** before talking about consequences if possible. Often consequences given in anger are humiliating and unreasonable.

- **If you can't think of a good consequence on the spot, and your child is four or older, buy time** by saying, "There will be a consequence for this. We'll discuss it later." Make a plan when your mind is clear or after you've consulted your partner or a friend. You may decide to enlist your child's help in choosing a consequence, or put it on the agenda for a family discussion. Remember to follow through: If you say there will be a consequence, make sure there is one. Younger children generally need to experience consequences more immediately. Use the direct-action strategy discussed in Chapter 7 and then plan ahead for the next time the problem occurs.

- **Expect your child to have a negative reaction to consequences,** especially if you are just beginning to introduce them. Consequences are not always pleasant, but they do give children valuable real-life lessons about the effects of their behavior. Your child may react with anger, whining, complaining, or crying. This is the child's right. Avoid confusing the situation by reacting to your child's negative response, which may reinforce the goal of getting attention. Simply state, in a neutral voice, "I can see that you are upset. Maybe you will choose differently next time," and then go about your business. Hold firm. It is very likely that your child will test you to see if you really mean what you say. In Chapter 11 we explore ways to help children deal with their anger.

- **If, after several incidents, your child isn't learning to behave differently as a result of the consequence, find another consequence, try another follow-through strategy, or switch to problem solving.**

- **Focus on your child's behavior rather than on his or her attitude.** What you want your child to do is probably not on his or her hit parade of fun things. It's unrealistic to expect to see a smiling face.

- **Avoid consequences that are punishing to you.** For instance, withholding the privilege of using the family car from the teenager who hauls younger siblings to games and lessons may not be in your best interest.

- **Children can be offered a choice between two consequences.** This gives them some power in the decision. Although they may not like either choice, they're more likely to cooperate when they participate in the process.

- **You don't need to use a consequence for every problem.** It's okay to warn the child that a behavior seems to be causing a problem without applying a consequence: "I've noticed that you've been forgetting to clean up the bathroom after you shower. The next time it happens, we'll have to think of a consequence."

Terry and Lois used their newly gained knowledge about consequences to handle a chronic problem:

Nine-year-old Mark was constantly losing his coat. He was on his third new coat of the school year, and it was only January. Frequently special trips were made to school to check the Lost and Found or to the soccer field or a friend's house where the elusive coat had been left. Terry was determined that they *weren't* going to spend money on another coat, and he nagged Mark mercilessly to get him to keep track of it.

Terry finally exploded out of frustration one morning when Mark announced that his coat was lost again. He let his son know that things were going to change, and he bought time to make a plan with Lois by telling Mark that they would discuss the problem that evening. Later he and Lois sat down together to come up with some ideas. They both agreed that in general Mark had trouble keeping track of all his things, but they decided to focus on the coat for now. Their nagging had escalated to the point that, rather than helping, it was creating a power struggle with Mark. Using the Three *R*s, Terry and Lois brainstormed consequences:

- If Mark left his coat somewhere, he would be grounded for a day.

- His allowance would be withheld if he lost his coat.

- He would be expected to pay for his coat if it was lost again.

- If the coat had to be retrieved by a parent, Mark would do a time trade.

- Mark would have to ride his bike back to wherever he had left his coat and retrieve it himself.

- Mark would have to wear a hand-me-down coat from his cousin if he lost the new one.

Terry felt that since the problem was already starting to feel like a power struggle, Mark might just ignore an order to retrieve the coat on his own. Also, some of the routes might not be safe biking for a nine-year-old. This option was not **reasonable** for the situation. The first two ideas were also scratched from the list because they weren't directly **related** to the problem. The remaining ideas were **reasonable, related,** and **respectful.**

Terry and Lois presented their plan to Mark that evening. They told him that they had decided to give him more responsibility for keeping track of his own coat. This time he would pay for half the purchase of a new coat. If he lost it again, he would have to pay for all of it. If he left the coat somewhere, he would have to figure out how to retrieve it himself.

Terry and Lois discussed this with Mark, helping him figure out how he might handle various situations. For instance, if he left it at a friend's house, he might call the friend and ask him to bring it to school the next day. In some situations, such as when he left the coat on the soccer field across town, they would need to drive him to get it. In these instances they would do a time trade: Mark would owe chore time of however much time it took to pick up the coat. If Mark lost his coat, he would have to wear the hand-me-down coat, which he wasn't particularly fond of, until he found his other coat or replaced it.

Mark complained that he was tired of being nagged about his coat. Terry and Lois agreed to stop reminding him repeatedly, but suggested that they use a one-word cue—"coat!"—when a memory jog was needed.

A few days later Mark was eating supper when he suddenly remembered that he'd left his new coat on the playground at school.

"What's your plan for taking care of it, Mark?" Lois responded.

"I'd better go to school a little early in the morning and check the Lost and Found," Mark suggested.

Mark wasn't very happy about getting up early the next morning, but he was less happy about the

prospect of having to wear a hand-me-down coat.
When he came home with his new coat after school, he
was obviously pleased with himself. The plan did hit a
few rough spots: The next week he lost *both* coats! But
Terry and Lois allowed natural consequences to teach
the lesson. Wearing three sweatshirts to school the
following cold morning motivated Mark to find the
stray coats, and his memory improved after that.

By using natural and logical consequences and by giving Mark
some choices about how he could handle the problem, Terry and
Lois deescalated the power struggle. They handed the problem
back to Mark: He could choose to forget his coat, but he would
have to take responsibility for the consequences of that choice.
Their recognition of the growing power struggle helped shape
their plan.

REFINING YOUR USE OF FOLLOW-THROUGH

Follow-through is more effective if it is shaped by an understanding of the reasons behind your child's behavior. According to
Rudolf Dreikurs, a pioneer of parent education, your emotional
response gives you clues to your child's motives. If you're *annoyed*
from continually having to remind or coax your child, he or she
may be seeking your involvement or *attention*. In this case consequences are a good choice because they reduce parental nagging, which removes the attention-getting benefit of this behavior.
Direct action might continue to encourage the behavior by feeding
the need for attention. Spend special time together to meet this
need. We'll discuss this and other strategies for emotional nurturing in Chapter 15.

In our experience sometimes the child who seeks attention is
also doing so out of a need to have clear limits or structure. Consequences combined with other follow-through strategies can be
an effective part of your intervention plan. When Susan's daughter,
Johanna, entered preschool at age three, she was clearly more independent than most kids her age—so independent that she'd
leave school and cross the street to play in the park whenever the
mood struck! Moreover Johanna quickly became the class clown,
seeming to have an insatiable need for attention from everyone
around her.

Her teachers' annoyance implied that Johanna needed the emotional nuturance provided by attention. Susan noticed her own irritation with her daughter, so she tried harder to meet Johanna's attention need. But her daughter seemed like an attention junkie, never getting enough special time from her parents. It wasn't until Johanna was seven that Susan discovered that her daughter's misdirected behavior was actually prompted by a need for *structure* rather than *nurture*. She and George used consequences to help establish more boundaries for Johanna. They also worked with her teacher to develop a plan for more structure at school. Within the next year Johanna calmed down considerably.

If you're feeling *angry* or challenged, rather than simply annoyed, your child may be hooking you in a *power struggle*. In this case the least possible intervention on your part makes the best sense. If a natural consequence isn't possible for the misdeed, take time to cool off and try problem solving with the child. If the situation is one that occurs often, such as bedtime problems, sit down and in a calm and friendly way discuss the difficulties the situation creates for you and the effect it has on the child: "I get really annoyed when you keep getting out of bed after I tuck you in. The time after you go to bed is my alone time, and I don't like to be interrupted unless there is an emergency. It makes bedtime really unpleasant for all of us. Tell me what this is like for you."

Enlist the child in choosing the consequences he prefers when the situation arises again: "What do you think I should do the next time this happens?" Then state clearly what you will do and leave it up to the child to decide his action, based on that information: "Each time you get out of bed, it interrupts my alone time. Tomorrow night you'll go to bed five minutes earlier for each interruption tonight so that you can pay me back my alone time."

Sometimes your angry feelings cover *hurt*, and you find yourself thinking, *How could you do this to me when I do so much for you?* The child may be trying to hurt you to seek *revenge* for something that you've done. Again, cooling off is an important first step in breaking this cycle. Problem solving will short-circuit the revenge cycle and involve children in decisions that affect them directly. You can speed up the process by keeping in mind the Three *R*s of consequences. Chapter 10 offers more details on problem solving with children.

Bear in mind that our emotional reactions may come from other sources altogether, such as leftover feelings from our own childhoods. Or we may have simply had a bad day at work. In addition kids need not have a deep underlying motive for every behavior.

A child who frequently forgets things may be one who is lost in his own world, by nature. Another child might be motivated by peer pressure. Sometimes children simply have different agendas than their parents. A preteen in the thick of an exciting video game may not be too happy when he is told it is time to get ready for bed. It is important for children to learn that they can't always do what they want. No matter what the motivation, it is our job to stretch them toward becoming more responsible as they move toward adulthood. Follow-through strategies are essential tools for doing this job.

TIME-OUT AND GROUNDING: CONSEQUENCE OR PUNISHMENT?

In recent years time-out has been used heavily by many parents as a follow-through strategy. The disadvantage of time-out for kids is that it is usually not related to the problem behavior, but instead is used as kind of blanket parental response when the child is behaving inappropriately. The child is taken (or ordered) away to be alone somewhere, removed from social interaction. Applied in this way, children experience time-out as a punishment, and they may focus on their anger or resentment at the parent rather than on the problem behavior.

Time-out can be a valuable tool, however, when parents relate it clearly to the problem. It makes sense when a child is being removed from a social situation because his behavior indicates that he can't be around people: "Because of the way you are acting, you will need to take a break in your room for a few minutes. When you are ready to stop hitting, you can rejoin us." A time-out might also be one way to deal with disruptive behavior at the dinner table. "One of our family rules is that we do not roughhouse during dinner. You lose the privilege of being with us until you can calm down. When you feel you are ready to stop roughhousing, you can join us again for dinner."

Time-out offers child and parent alike the opportunity to be alone to cool off or to get centered. In fact sometimes it's the parent who needs a time-out, but it's the child who is isolated. As a last resort this is a useful strategy for getting a cooling-off break from a child who is driving you toward a blowup. In some situations, such as when you have other small children to attend to, you can't take a time out for yourself. If this is the case, it helps to be honest with the child: "I need you to go to your room for a few minutes. I'm getting angry, and I need a break. When I'm feeling better, we'll talk about it.''

Unfortunately sometimes our tone of voice and words give the message that we're using time-out as a punishment rather than as a consequence. As you give a simple explanation of the time-out and how it is connected to the problem behavior, be as firm and kind as possible.

The same rule of thumb also applies to grounding, which is the strategy parents most often overuse with older kids. Parents ground their teens as a follow-through strategy when they want to exercise their parental authority. Unfortunately it has the same limitations as time-out. Unless it's connected to the behavior of the child, it becomes another generic form of punishment that is frequently overused. As one teenager complained, "My parents used time-out until I was ten and then they started grounding me for everything. Can't they be a little more creative?"

Instead of resorting to grounding, express your strong disapproval of the child's action and then buy time to come up with a related consequence. You might still decide to ground him, but you'll have time to consider whether this consequence is suitable and relevant to the transgression:

Because of the rough kids who hung out there, the neighborhood convenience store had been off-limits to Fred's children since before they were teenagers. Since Fred was at work in the afternoons, he laid down some clear rules about what activities were appropriate when the children were home in the hours after school. Coming home early one day, he happened to drive past the forbidden store. Out front was his thirteen-year-old, Joe, with a group of other kids.

When his son walked in the door later that afternoon, Fred was steaming. He told Joe what he'd seen and let him know that there would be a consequence for his behavior. After thinking about his options, Fred decided that grounding his son would be the best consequence.

Once he'd cooled off, he called Joe in and said, "We have a clear family rule about hanging out at Zippy Mart. Since you weren't able to handle the freedom I gave you after school, you lose the privilege of being away from the house. You're grounded in the afternoons until I get home, for two weeks.

CONSISTENCY OR RIGIDITY?

When we hear the parenting admonition "Be consistent," most of us assume it means that we should treat all children equally and respond the same way in all discipline situations. If we adhere to this view of consistency, not only do we fail to honor the differences in the needs of individual children but we also risk becoming boxed in and rigid in our responses to conflict. Often a creative or unexpected response to a child's unacceptable behavior will change the course of action and decrease the power struggles. For example, at her office Jeanne found a notepad with a hooded executioner holding an ax. The caption read, "**DO IT OR ELSE.**" She brought a sheet of it home. The next time Andy forgot to clean his room, she taped the message to his door and signed it. When he saw it, they both had a good laugh, and Andy started in on his room.

In addition the belief that we must be perfectly consistent is a burden that we don't need as parents. We can easily burn out or give up setting limits if it takes too much work. We *do* need to be consistent about doing *something* to follow through, however! Otherwise children very quickly learn that we don't mean what we say and will respond accordingly. This kind of consistency takes self-discipline, determination, support, and lots of practice. Fortunately we don't need to make up situations for practice. Our daily lives hand us these opportunities in abundance!

Practicing

1. Think of a time when you asked your child to do something and were left with a feeling of powerlessness when she didn't cooperate. Pick two follow-through strategies you might have used to change your child's response.

2. In the chart of sample consequences that follows, find an example for each of these types of consequences:

• Loss or delay of privilege

• Loss or delay of cooperation

• Compensation

3. For each example below choose whether you would use direct action, natural consequences, or logical consequences, and explain why:

Tony, eleven, leaves his bike in the front yard when he goes to bed.
Sarah, five, "forgets" to wash her hands before dinner.
Donna, seven, frequently leaves toys strewn around the living room.
Jim, twelve, comes home an hour late from his friend's house several times in a row.

4. Offer each of the above children a choice. ("Either you _____ or _____," or "When you _____, then _____.")

5. Think of a specific situation with a child when you could have been more effective in following through. Using the information you just learned, how might you react differently the next time? Close your eyes and envision yourself in the situation sometime in the next few days. Imagine what you'll say and how your kids might react. Share your experience with your partner or a friend. Try out the new response and report how it went.

82

Sample Consequences

Use this chart as a starting point to generate a variety of consequences. *Consequences need to be adapted to your child's age and to the specific situation.*

PROBLEM BEHAVIOR	CONSEQUENCE
Refusal to eat the food served at meals	"You'll need to eat what I cook for you, or you can fix yourself a sandwich."
Chores not done by agreed-upon time	"You can eat dinner after you empty the trash." "The TV can be turned on when the chores are done." "We won't be able to go roller skating since you didn't get your chores done in time to be ready to leave before the rink closes."
Difficulty getting settled at bedtime	"Since you've called me to your room three times tonight, you'll need to pay back my time tomorrow by doing some chores for me."

PROBLEM BEHAVIOR	CONSEQUENCE
Not ready when it's time to leave for school	"It's time to go. You'll need to get in the car even if you're not ready." "I'm sorry you chose to be late for school today. It's too bad you'll be marked down as being tardy." "I'm sorry you were late and missed the bus today. You'll need to walk or ride your bike."
Difficulty getting out of bed in the morning	"Since you had so much trouble getting out of bed this morning, it seems like you didn't get enough sleep last night. Tonight you'll need to go to bed a half hour earlier."
Fighting or other rowdy behavior in the car	"Since I can't drive with so much racket going on, I'm parking the car until you settle down."
Rude behavior toward an adult (disrespectful language or physical actions)	"I don't deserve to be called names, and I'm leaving the room. Let me know when you're ready to talk to me differently."

PROBLEM BEHAVIOR	CONSEQUENCE
Temper tantrums in store	"We'll need to leave the store since you're not controlling your behavior." "I'm sorry you won't be going with me to the store next time, since you didn't control your behavior this time."
Teeth not brushed	"Since you are not brushing your teeth regularly, you won't be able to eat sweets. If you brush your teeth regularly for a week without reminders, we'll discuss it again."
Not staying down at naptime	"If you don't stay quiet in your room, you're choosing to go to bed right after dinner tonight."
Items left around the house	"If you can't remember to pick up your crayons and toys, I'll have to put them away for a few days." "Since I had to pick up your toys from the dining-room floor, you owe me some work time."
Loses, damages, or breaks objects belonging to others	"Since you left your brother's book out in the rain, you'll need to replace it."

PROBLEM BEHAVIOR	CONSEQUENCE
Loses, damages, or breaks objects belonging to self	"I'm sorry you broke your doll. I guess you won't be able to play with it anymore since it's broken."
Living room messy	"When you mess up the living room like this, you lose the privilege of using it for a day." "Since I cleaned up your mess in the living room while you were at school, you owe me some work time."
Sibling fights at mealtime	"When the fighting stops, we'll continue with dinner."
Arriving home later than the agreed-on time	"Since you arrived home late from your friend's house, you will lose the privilege of going out after school for the rest of the week."
Missed lessons or classes	"Since you forgot to go to your aikido class, you will need to pay me back for the cost (or part of the cost) of the class."

PART TWO

Using C.H.O.I.C.E.S. to Resolve Conflicts

"If the only tools you have are hammers, every problem begins to look like a nail."

—*Abraham Maslow*

6

C.H.O.I.C.E.S. for Managing Conflict

"The stuff my parents did doesn't work with my kids. Sometimes I feel so helpless when I try to discipline them. When I'm on the spot, I just can't think of what to do. I usually end up getting mad and yelling my head off."

—*Rick, parent of three*

THIS PARENT DESCRIBES THE POWERLESSNESS MANY OF US FEEL AS WE search for ways to respond to conflicts with our kids. We've probably used some strategies a great deal—particularly those that match our conflict-resolution styles. But approaches that have more in common with other conflict styles may seem foreign to us. If we expand our choices, we will feel more capable of handling the variety of situations that our kids present us. That's why the two of us put our heads together, applied our collective experience of thirty-plus years dealing with kids and their conflicts, and created C.H.O.I.C.E.S., a collection of practical strategies for handling conflicts between adults and children and between children. You'll probably recognize your favorite strategies in the list. By working with the C.H.O.I.C.E.S. in this chapter and those that follow, you'll refine old strategies and discover new ones.

USING C.H.O.I.C.E.S. TO SET LIMITS

Children need limits in order to feel physically and emotionally safe. Using C.H.O.I.C.E.S. for limit setting allows for a broad range of differences in children's temperament and development. Parents also have a range of personality styles and temperaments, just as kids do. As you explore the C.H.O.I.C.E.S. chapters, you'll begin to expand on your old ways of handling conflicts with your kids, and you'll develop new flexibility. For now look through the list and recognize your old favorites. You may find that techniques you've come to rely on in the past will be even more effective in the future when used as one of a *variety* of strategies for responding to conflict.

C.H.O.I.C.E.S. for Managing Conflict

- COMMAND: Giving clear directions; specifically stating what you want the child to do in a nonhumiliating manner: "Clean up your room before visiting your friend."

- HUMOR OR SURPRISE: Using nonsarcastic humor or doing the unexpected can defuse an explosive situation. Channel kids who are bickering over a toy into a different activity: "Let's pretend we're robots and clean up the family room."

- OFFER CHOICES: Giving a choice between two options: "You can _____ or _____," or "When you _____, then you can _____."

- IGNORE: Choosing not to address the conflict or unacceptable behavior by withholding attention.

- COMPROMISE: Seeking a middle ground by finding a solution that partially satisfies both parties: "If you _____, then I'll _____."

- ENCOURAGE PROBLEM SOLVING: Working together to explore the disagreement, generate alternatives, and find a solution that satisfies the needs of both parties: "What can we do to meet everyone's needs?"

- STRUCTURE THE ENVIRONMENT: Rearranging people, room structure, or objects to reduce conflict: separate kids who are fighting in the car by moving them to different seats.

C.H.O.I.C.E.S. can be used alone or in combination, as one parent, Julie, discovered as she worked on the messy-room dilemma with her ten-year-old son, Greg:

Julie began her campaign by announcing to Greg that he had to clean his room once a week (**commanding**). This was her nonnegotiable limit. He could choose the day when he'd do the task (**offering choices**). They spent time together in Greg's room solving various organizational problems (**problem solving**). A trash can and a dirty-clothes hamper were added, and Greg rearranged his shelf and storage space (**structuring the environment**). Julie encouraged Greg to make the organizational decisions that would help him keep his room clean.

For several weeks Greg cleaned up his room regularly on Saturdays. When he began to neglect this task, Julie instituted a "when you _____, then you may _____" follow-through strategy. Greg could go out to play after his room was cleaned up on Saturdays (**offering choices**).

Over the months Julie noticed several changes in Greg's behavior. He started insisting that his friends help clean up after playing in his room. He also began to put dirty clothes in the hamper, so the room was much less messy when cleaning day came on Saturday. While Greg's room is still not absolutely tidy, he has become more aware of his habits and is beginning to take more responsibility for its tidiness. Julie still has to enforce the Saturday-noon cleaning deadline, and Greg sometimes grumbles or complains, but they have made significant progress on the issue. Only occasionally does she resort to posting a sign on his door that declares his room a hazardous waste dump (**surprise or humor**).

Julie was particularly skillful at combining strategies. She enlisted Greg's cooperation by involving him in decisions about the organization of his room. As a result he was more likely to take responsibility for its condition.

USING C.H.O.I.C.E.S. TO GENERATE NEW SOLUTIONS TO OLD PROBLEMS

In our classes we suggest that people look at the C.H.O.I.C.E.S. list to spark their creativity in solving long-standing problems. For example, one parent brought up the problem of her son constantly leaving his coat and backpack on the living-room couch. Here are some of the ideas we generated by using the C.H.O.I.C.E.S. list:

- **Command:** "Pick up your coat and backpack *now*," or a one-word cue, "Backpack." If necessary, use follow-through: Gently lead him by the arm over to his coat and backpack.

- **Humor, surprise:** Stand waiting like a personal valet when the child enters.

- **Offer choices:** "You can pick up your coat now, or I'll pick it up and you'll owe me a job later."

- **Ignore:** Leave the coat there and don't worry about it.

- **Compromise:** "You pick up your coat, and I'll pick up your backpack."

- **Encourage problem solving:** Sit down with your son, discuss the issue, and problem-solve together.

- **Structure the environment:** Put up hooks at kid level for coats and backpacks.

TIPS FOR USING C.H.O.I.C.E.S.

- **Be careful if you are very angry.** We do not make our best parenting decisions when we're furious, to put it mildly. Buy time to cool off: "I need to calm down and think about what to do about this, and I'll get back to you later."

- **The way you say it is important.** Be firm and kind. Remember to support your child's self-esteem by being respectful in the way you discipline him. Instead of saying, "You dummy, I've told you a million times to stay out of the street," you might try, "Your feet need to be on the sidewalk now. It's not safe to play in the street." Let your face and body speak, as well as your words. Get in touch with your caring feelings as you set limits.

- **Have a plan.** When you have a situation that is constantly a problem with your child (bedtime, cleaning up, getting dressed), make a plan for how you will deal with it in the future. In a calm moment away from the situation brainstorm C.H.O.I.C.E.S. strategies that are practical for you and reasonable and respectful to your child.

• **Keep at it.** You can expect your child to test you to see if you mean it. The unacceptable behavior may increase before you see improvement. Don't give up before you can see the benefits of your efforts.

HOW TO USE THE REST OF THIS BOOK

The chapters that follow will guide you in developing your own personal discipline framework using C.H.O.I.C.E.S. The information from the conflict-management inventory in Chapter 2 will help you decide which strategies to focus on. Read all the chapters first and then give special attention to those that will complement your dominant style or styles.

For example, if you've been an **avoider** or an **accommodator**, Chapter 7 provides strategies that will help you set limits and respond to conflict more directly. If **directing** has been your strong style, focus on the strategies that will give your children more opportunities for decision making. You'll also find it helpful to read about **collaboration** in Chapter 10; and Chapters 8 and 9 on **compromise** and **avoiding** will give you alternatives to direct confrontation.

Use the chart below to guide you in selecting C.H.O.I.C.E.S. chapters that will enhance your collection of parenting tools:

DIRECTOR	COLLABORATOR	COMPROMISER	ACCOMMODATOR	AVOIDER
Compromising (Ch. 8)	Directing (Ch. 7)	Directing (Ch. 7)	Directing (Ch. 7)	Directing (Ch. 7)
Avoiding (Ch. 9)	Compromising (Ch. 8)	Avoiding (Ch. 9)	Compromising (Ch. 8)	Compromising (Ch. 8)
Collaborating (Ch. 10)	Avoiding (Ch. 9)	Collaborating (Ch. 10)	Collaborating (Ch. 10)	Collaborating (Ch. 10)

If you're comfortable with the discipline structure you have in place, work toward developing the problem-solving strategy outlined in Chapter 10. This approach encourages decision-making skills that will help your children develop responsible, caring behavior. You'll be preparing the canvas for the *peaceable* family of the next generation.

Practicing

1. Find an example of each of the C.H.O.I.C.E.S. from your own or someone else's parenting. Which do you use most frequently? Which do you see others use most frequently?
2. Post the C.H.O.I.C.E.S. list in a place where you'll see it often. Notice which strategies come easily for you and which ones are more awkward as you explore new ways and revisit old ones.

7

Directing Strategies for Telling Them Straight: Command and Offer Choices

Sandra was a parent of two children, ages two and four. Her four-year-old daughter, Cassie, had undergone hip surgery in infancy and was in leg casts when most other children her age were learning to walk. Because of Cassie's disability, Sandra protected and indulged her by doing things for her that she was capable of doing herself. Unfortunately this pattern continued after her daughter had recovered.

Cassie became a clinging, dependent preschooler, demanding that her mother dress and feed her. Sandra began to see that she needed to encourage independence in her daughter. Cassie resisted by throwing temper tantrums and refusing to do anything at all. Sandra felt guilty because she was beginning to resent her daughter, so she tried pleading with Cassie to do more things for herself. Cassie refused to comply, ignoring Sandra's repeated requests. The more Sandra asked, the better Cassie got at ignoring her. Eventually Sandra could only get Cassie's attention when her anger and frustration got the best of her and she screamed at her daughter. This proved no more effective than when she had been nice and reasonable. After long, stressful days with Cassie, Sandra would fall into bed exhausted. Despite her growing irritation with

Cassie, most of the time she continued to overprotect her daughter physically and emotionally. When her doctor told her she was developing ulcers, Sandra realized she was in a crisis of ineffectiveness.

THE POLITENESS THAT HAD ALWAYS WORKED SO WELL IN OTHER AREAS OF Sandra's life was lost on her daughter. Cassie needed Sandra to be firm and clear about what behavior she expected and to follow through.

Sandra was surprised that her daughter wouldn't behave properly just to please her mother. She had assumed that Cassie would learn to be respectful simply by being treated respectfully at home. Sandra was afraid that it was unreasonable to tell her daughter what to do without taking into account Cassie's feelings or wishes. She didn't realize that she could tell Cassie what to do while still validating her daughter's feelings: "I know you're angry, *and* you'll still need to . . ."

Eventually Sandra's unmet expectations surfaced in angry ultimatums. She found herself saying things like, "I thought you had better sense than that," or "How could you be so stupid?" Even when she managed to set limits without yelling at Cassie, blame and humiliation were just below the surface.

For an **accommodator** or **avoider** like Sandra, it takes practice to develop the skill of making direct statements and taking decisive action. Our parenting group helped Sandra target frustrating situations and practice directing responses. She planned consequences and mentally rehearsed her reactions to specific touchy situations. Once she felt prepared, she tackled the problem head on. When Cassie refused to get ready for school in the morning, instead of trying to cajole her into cooperating Sandra gave her a command followed up with a consequence: "You need to get dressed now. We'll be leaving at eight, and if you're not ready, you'll be going to school as you are." Sandra made it through the initial awkward period of change, using self-talk to keep herself cool and to remind herself of how important this change was. This also helped her to follow through when Cassie threw a tantrum in protest. Gradually Cassie began to find that her old methods weren't working, and she became less demanding and more independent.

WHAT IS COMMANDING?

Commanding sounds like a military order, but a command is really no more than a clear, direct, authoritative statement of the behavior we expect the person to carry out: "You need to wash your hands before you sit down for dinner." "It's time to clean up the kitchen." "You need to hold a grown-up's hand when you cross the street." When we command, we assume our appropriate parental role of protecting and supporting our children. We set the limits children need to feel safe and secure. We enlist their help with daily tasks, help them learn responsibility, and teach them to follow directions.

WHEN TO USE COMMANDING

Commanding is necessary with younger children, where safety concerns are foremost. As children get older, however, they need more opportunities to practice solving problems. Although commanding is sometimes essential, it is often not as effective as other approaches for adolescents or for strong-willed children, for whom a command can be a call to a battle that neither the parent nor the child wins. Commands used judiciously, *with appropriate follow-through,* can still be effective.

TIPS FOR COMMANDING

Regardless of the maturity or personality of your child, the following guidelines will improve your chances for success in directing him or her:

- **State clearly the desirable (and undesirable) behavior.** Make sure your child is aware of what the inappropriate behavior is. "It's not okay to kick your brother. Use your words to tell him that you don't like it when he goes into your room without knocking."

- **Use the command strategy sparingly.** If we overuse the command strategy, children will tune us out. Save it for the situations when it's most needed.

- **Give expectations firmly but kindly.** Unfortunately many people have difficulty giving a command to their child until they are up against the wall and feeling furious and frustrated. It's hard to command kindly and respectfully when we're operating from anger. Try to be clear and firm about your expectations: "I expect you to have the lawn mowed by noon." Do this *before* you reach the boiling point, or buy time until you've cooled off.

- **Acknowledge your child's viewpoint by agreeing whenever you can and by recognizing his or her feelings while sticking to your agenda.** "Yes, you're right. Your sister *does* get to stay up later than you do, *and* when you get to be thirteen, you'll be able to stay up later too," or "I can see that you're really upset because your teacher asked you to do this paper over again, *and* you need to do it now, before the TV can go on." Use *and* instead of *but* in order to avoid sending the message that you're discounting your child's viewpoint.

- **Make eye contact with your child.** Eyes communicate. Many children need a visual and a verbal message. It's helpful for younger children if you physically get down on their level and say, "I need your eyes." If you're dealing with a six-and-a-half-foot teenager, you may need to suggest that you both sit down to establish eye contact.

- **Avoid nagging.** When we hear our exasperated voices repeat the same instructions over and over, we can be pretty sure that our kids hear it as nagging. Many of us can remember from our own childhoods how ineffective it is to be told to do something repeatedly. Why should children listen if they know it's going to be said again and again?

- **Be prepared to follow through if your child doesn't respond.** To avoid nagging, make a plan about how you'll follow through if your children don't respond to your directive. They need to know that you mean what you say and that you will either take direct action or provide a consequence. "You need to put on your helmet and wrist protectors before you go skating. If you use your skates without protective equipment, you'll lose the privilege of using them for the rest of the day."

OFFERING CHOICES

Most other parents would have gladly traded their strong-willed child for one who was as pliable as Megan. Lucy and Patrick's six-year-old daughter was unusually acquiescent in matters of discipline. When Megan began to assume the victim role on the playground, however, Lucy and Patrick became concerned that their daughter wasn't learning to be assertive. They also wanted to help Megan develop problem-solving skills. They decided to stop using time-outs in response to transgressions and instead offered Megan *a choice* between doing what her parents asked and a consequence. By using consequences instead of time-out at home, two things happened: The emphasis changed from punishment for being bad to consequences for poor decisions. It also provided Megan with training in voicing her preferences. Lucy and Patrick took every opportunity to give Megan choices: between taking out the trash or clearing the table after dinner; between reading a book together or playing a game. Although she was timid at first, Megan gradually began to be comfortable communicating her desires. This was a first step in teaching Megan to stand up for herself.

When we offer children a choice, we give them more power than when we give a straight command, and we help teach them to make decisions at the same time. Simple choices may be offered to children as young as toddlers.

The simplest form of choice is to offer children two options only: **"You may _____ or _____."** This strategy is particularly effective for dealing with picky eaters: "Would you prefer apple or orange juice to drink?" carefully avoids mention of root beer, ginger ale, or a host of other beverages you may not wish your child to have, and yet it allows the child some room for preference. Allow younger children simple choices between foods or among play activities. As children become older, this is a powerful directing strategy: "You can practice the piano or write your thank-you notes this morning."

Choices between consequences, described in Chapter 5, is another form of offering choices: "You can play in *our* yard, or you can come in the house for the rest of the day." This enlists our kids in owning their behavior *and* its consequences.

WHEN TO OFFER CHOICES

Offering simple choices gives support to children who get overwhelmed and confused by too many possibilities. "To begin cleaning your room, would you like to pick up the clothes on the floor or make your bed?" will get better results than "Clean your room."

It is especially useful for children who need direction but who would balk at giving up their own voice totally.

MAKING DIRECTING STRATEGIES STICK BY FOLLOWING THROUGH

Unfortunately offering polite direction or a simple choice isn't a magic wand for eliciting desired behavior in our children. We may need to add clout to the choice through the use of consequences or direct action. *Effective follow-through is the key to successful directing.*

Practicing

1. During the next week notice situations where the use of a command statement would be effective. Think of commands that will give your child a clear message about what behavior you expect. Describe the inappropriate behavior and the desired behavior. Remember to make eye contact and to say it kindly but firmly. Plan your follow-through strategy and be ready to act. Expect resistance, and hang in there.

2. Plan ahead for a time when you can apply the choice strategy: "You may _____ or _____." If your child argues or tries to ignore your request, repeat it until he agrees to one of the choices.

8

Compromising Strategies: Giving Without Giving Up

Alice was in the kitchen preparing for a class she was teaching as she cooked French toast for her five-year-old daughter, Lisa. She delivered the meal to the dining room, and in a minute the call came, "Mom, please cut the crusts off." Cutting off the crusts was a long-standing tradition that was getting old to Alice, and at that moment she was especially engrossed in her work and didn't want to be bothered. Nor did she wish to begin to work on changing her daughter's behavior.

"You cut the crusts off the first one with your table knife, then I'll come and cut the crusts off the second in a few minutes," she offered.

Lisa agreed, and Alice was able to finish writing down her thoughts before she went in to help her daughter. She noted that she'd need to make a plan to change this annoying ritual.

WITHOUT EVEN REALIZING IT, MOST OF US MAKE COUNTLESS PRODUCTIVE compromises at home or at work on small issues that aren't important enough to negotiate. Those who are most successful in using this strategy know when the issue is minor enough that they can let go of getting all of their own needs met. Each side gives up something in a compromise, but each side also gets something. The compromise strategy bought Alice the few minutes she needed to finish her work, and it also partially met Lisa's need for her mom's attention.

COMPROMISE: A BASIC ELEMENT OF PARTNERSHIP

Give-and-take is important in all satisfying personal relationships. Increasingly employers emphasize effective teamwork on the job. When we use compromise as a way of resolving conflicts between children, we're teaching them a valuable team skill.

It's important for children to know that they can't get everything they want. It's also good for them to practice giving up some things to get others. When we compromise, we share our power with the child, forging partnerships with give-and-take. Compromise can be an antidote to unnecessary power struggles.

In order for a compromise to be effective, the players must be clear about what trade-offs they are willing to make and which principles are nonnegotiable. Bob's sixteen-year-old son, Brett, wanted to stay out with his friends all night after the prom. Bob felt that no sixteen-year-old was ready for the responsibility of being out on his own all night. For him this was nonnegotiable. He did, however, agree to have Brett's friends over for a post-prom breakfast.

When we remain firm about our own bottom line, we are demonstrating personal integrity. By agreeing to compromise, we're recognizing our children's opinions and feelings through listening and finding a satisfying middle ground. We're also establishing a middle ground between the extremes of overdirecting and habitual avoidance or accommodation.

Richard, who was a recovering **accommodator** and **avoider,** leaned out the upstairs window and hollered for his kids to come in and start getting ready for bed. They were having a glorious time playing a game with several neighborhood kids. Richard's request was met by a storm of protest. He paused for a moment and considered his options. In the past he would have taken another half hour of peace to get his work done and eventually corralled his kids at the last minute. By doing this he avoided their protests, but a rushed bedtime routine was usually the result. Richard decided to change his usual avoidance pattern and try the **compromise** strategy. He wanted to make bedtime calmer, but he also wanted to give the kids a little more time outdoors, since they were playing together so well. "You can have five more minutes if you agree to come in without a fuss," he called.

"Okay!" came the response.

Richard told them when the five minutes were up, but they didn't believe him, based on his previous lack of follow-through. They continued to play. Richard then applied **direct action** by going outside and ushering each child in by the arm. The second time this issue arose, the children responded with only a minor protest. The third time they surprised him by complying immediately. Since then the coming-in-when-called issue takes considerably less of Richard's emotional energy, and he's found that getting the kids to bed smoothly gives him the bonus of extra personal time. He's given his kids and himself a gift.

WHEN TO USE COMPROMISE

Compromise is a useful strategy for children of any stage, although very young children may need help remembering their end of the compromise. Whenever possible, insist that a younger child follow through on his part of the bargain first, *before* you honor your part. This will help avoid the confrontation and frustrations spawned by a broken agreement.

Many clashes between teenagers and parents can be defused by compromise, which honors the teenager's need to be different from the person in authority.

Shouting matches had been going for a full year over Jennifer's use of the phone. She begged her family to buy her her own phone for her thirteenth birthday. Her parents, however, had no intention of paying the monthly bill for two lines. The battle lines were drawn until they hit upon a **compromise:** Jennifer would be given an extension phone, and the family would add Call Waiting to their current phone service. When Jennifer chatted with her friends and heard the tone indicating that another caller was trying to get through, she would hang up, allowing her parents to speak to their party. The additional cost on the monthly bill would be split between Jennifer and her parents.

Jennifer's mom and dad showed respect for her need to use the phone without losing sight of their own needs in the process. They also gave Jennifer responsibility in helping to come up with a solution and in carrying it out. After ironing out the kinks in the new system, everyone involved benefited from the improved relations.

Tips for Compromising

Some handy hints will help you avoid difficulties with compromise:

- **Before offering to compromise, be sure you can give up part of what you want.** Work on recognizing the difference between negotiable and nonnegotiable issues.

- **State your ideal position aloud before suggesting a compromise position.** "What I would like is for you to mow the lawn every Saturday morning. I'm willing to let you decide when you do it, as long as it's done once a week." Kids need to see clearly what each person is giving up. This also helps you avoid the resentment that comes from compromising twice, once before your position is stated and once in negotiation.

- **Avoid unspoken compromises.** Be careful not to make the mistaken assumption that if you give up something now, your child will be more likely to cooperate with you at some future time. Kids (and most adults) don't think this way, and you'll probably end up feeling resentful.

- **Children who are reluctant to cooperate can be given a choice between agreeing to the compromise and being told what to do by the parent.**

- **When possible, have children follow through on their part of the bargain first.** It's easy to suggest a compromise and then forget to collect on your part of the bargain. Help younger kids remember their agreement.

- **Be careful not to overuse this strategy.** Some children may become quite skillful at luring you into a compromise when you need to set a clear limit. *Warning: Habitual compromising can disguise conflict avoidance.*

Practicing

1. Think of compromises for the following situations:

Chuck, age eight, wants hot lunches every day at school. His dad wants him to take bag lunches for reasons of economy and nutrition.

Nikki, age fifteen, refuses to wear any athletic shoes but one brand, which happens to be the most expensive.

Emily, age seven, repeatedly calls her mother to her room for various requests every night after lights are out at bedtime.

Dennis, nine, and Sandy, six, each claim that the prize in the cereal box should be theirs.

2. The next time you're in a conflict situation with your child, buy time. Think about what is negotiable and what is nonnegotiable for you. Then discuss the problem with your child and find a compromise solution.

9

Avoiding Strategies: Artfully Ignoring, Using Humor, Taking Them by Surprise, or Structuring the Environment

Five-year-old Tara's grandmother was at her wits' end. They were traveling together and were due to meet some friends for breakfast in five minutes. Tara seemed to have rolled out of bed on the wrong side that morning. She brought the dressing routine to a halt by tearfully refusing all three pairs of pants in her suitcase. Tara's grandmother took a deep breath and did a few seconds of creative thinking. Then she burst into an animated version of "eeny, meeny, miney moe," pointing to each pair of pants as she proceeded with the chant. Tara's resistance dissolved as she was caught up in her grandmother's playful strategy. The pants were chosen as the chant ended, and they got on with their day.

HUMOROUS STRATEGIES ARE MADE TO ORDER FOR THIS KIND OF TICKLISH situation, because they head off a confrontation by rechanneling inappropriate behavior playfully. You may be thinking, *Wait a minute. After all this talk about overcoming conflict avoidance, you're telling me that it's okay to use humor to avoid a problem?*

Throughout the book we've repeatedly cited overavoidance of conflict as a major source of difficulty. And now we're advising avoidance as a discipline strategy. Why? Because by *consciously* choosing to steer away from confrontation, we are turning avoidance into a tool for conflict management. This is not the same as playing ostrich as a reactive habit, nor does it deny the existence of the conflict. It's the denial of conflict or the overuse of avoidance that causes problems, not the avoidance approach itself. When dealing with teenagers, for instance, focusing on the bigger issues and ignoring small irritations can be a key to peaceable survival.

WHAT IS THE IGNORING STRATEGY?

Most of us unconsciously use ignoring as a coping strategy with our kids. We instinctively ignore many insignificant yet annoying behaviors, such as when kids squabble in the living room over the rules of a game. Even after the behavior surfaces in our awareness and we need to decide how to respond, sometimes the best choice is to continue to ignore it. When we consciously ignore a problem our kids have created, we may be sending them a vote of confidence: "I know that you can handle it yourselves."

> Charles complained that his four children were constantly bickering. He often intervened to bring peace back to the house. No sooner did he turn his back, however, than the bickering began again. After several frustrating encounters like this, the usual result was Charles blowing up and sending the kids to separate rooms. Charles eventually came to realize that a certain amount of squabbling was normal for a family of six living in close quarters. Since there was no danger of physical violence, he could ignore much of it. He also learned that sometimes the kids created a ruckus to get his attention. They knew from experience that it was an easy way to get him involved with them.
>
> In a calm moment he informed his kids that he would no longer allow himself to be sucked into their bickering, and he expressed his confidence in their ability to handle the small stuff. Knowing that the likelihood of physical violence was low, he chose to remove himself from center stage and to retreat to his room the next time the fracas started to annoy him. His kids eventually did get better at solving their disagreements without him. The practice they'd had

using problem-solving skills in family meetings was paying off. Charles had the wisdom to realize that it's important not to ignore conflicts or expect children to handle things for themselves without giving them the skills they need to deal with them.

WHEN AND HOW TO USE IGNORING

Pairing ignoring with a direct command and a probable consequence is especially effective with children who are prone to power struggles:

> Seven-year-old Sam had the habit of throwing temper tantrums or engaging his mother in power struggles when things weren't going his way. He usually met bathtime with a storm of protest: "It's not fair. . . . I just had a bath last night. . . . I'm *not* going to take a bath." His mother, who was exploring ways to eliminate the tantrums, decided to respond matter-of-factly, "I'm not impressed by your temper tantrum, so you can stop anytime." She turned back to the sink and continued doing the dishes.
> She waited for the angry display that followed to play itself out. Then she went to Sam's room, where he had retreated. He immediately greeted her with a list of reasons why he shouldn't have to bathe that night. Instead of engaging in her usual comebacks and getting caught in crossfire, his mom calmly said, "You need to be in the tub within the next ten minutes," and quietly walked out of the room. Sam knew from his recent experiences of his mother's follow-through that her instructions wouldn't be forgotten. Sam's mom gave him some control in the situation by allowing him ten minutes, but she also gave him a clear message about the result she expected. Then she simply ignored Sam's call to battle by removing herself from the scene. Ten minutes later Sam was in the tub.

Children who engage in temper tantrums usually respond well to ignoring strategies. Naming the unacceptable behavior, indicating your disapproval, and then ignoring it is often effective. Some children (particularly younger ones who want attention more than power) will rage for a few minutes, and then the display is over. Ignoring the outburst removes the attention and part of the motivation for the tantrum.

Sometimes, though, the child will continue to escalate the tantrum until you're forced to become involved. If your child tends to do this, it's better not to use the ignoring strategy. A tantrum might be the child's way of asking for clearer limits, so it's helpful to back up ignoring with consequences. It's important to recognize that your child may also be acting out to get your attention. Plan special time, as discussed in Chapter 14. We'll explore more ideas for dealing with kids' anger in Chapter 11.

Another proven tactic for ignoring protest and argument is the broken-record technique. This is an effective strategy for the "lawyer child" who tries to argue you out of perfectly reasonable requests.

> Jenny noticed that her ten-year-old son, Justin, was wearing the same shirt for the third day in a row.
> "Justin, you need to change your shirt. You've had it on for three days now, and it needs to go in the wash."
> "Uh-uh. I just put it on last night."
> "You need to change your shirt now."
> "I like it this way. It feels good when it's stretchy."
> "You need to change your shirt now."
> "It doesn't even look dirty."
> "You need to change your shirt now."

If Justin responded to Jenny's request with an angry outburst, she might have come back with, "I can see that you're angry about having to change your shirt since you really like it so much. *And* you need to put on a clean shirt now." This acknowledges his feelings, but at the same time shows that she refuses to be sidetracked by his protests. This kind of child can learn to hone his critical-thinking skills elsewhere. For instance, involving a lawyer child in problem solving puts his talents to good use. Read more about engaging children in problem solving in Chapter 10.

USING SURPRISE AND HUMOR STRATEGIES

Surprise and humor strategies distract kids from conflicts. These solutions are usually creative or unpredictable ways of avoiding confrontation. Apply your parental ingenuity to make the surprise strategy work. You may surprise *yourself* with the ideas you can think of in a pinch.

TAKING THEM BY SURPRISE

A couple of summers ago we were about to leave our families to attend a week-long workshop, and we decided to take our daughters out for a guilt-reducing ice-cream cone. It was the end of a long, busy day, and everyone was tired. In the car five-year-old Anna Marie insisted on sitting next to her mother. Jeanne strapped her in the seat belt in the backseat and climbed in the front, thinking Anna Marie would forget about her wishes as soon as they got under way. Instead the complaining and crying escalated until it was clear that something had to be done. Just loudly enough to be heard over the crying, Jeanne murmured, "Anna Marie, bottlenugget."

Anna Marie's crying stopped. "What?" she said.

"Bottlenugget."

"What's that?"

Jeanne commenced a long, fictitious story about three-foot-long ants called bottlenuggets who live on ice-cream cones and like to do jump-rope tricks with kids. Soon all of us were spinning the tall tale of the bottlenuggets and their friends. Anna Marie's woes were forgotten, and everyone was entertained in the process.

Diverting children's energies into another activity is a tried-and-true surprise strategy for avoiding conflict.

For most of the morning, three-year-old Maggie and her eight-year-old brother, Paul, were bickering over whether to use blocks for a castle or a fort. Their mother, Carla, decided that it was time to intervene when their voices escalated and violence appeared to be imminent. "Let's get out the watercolors and paint some pictures for Gramps!" she enthusiastically suggested. From experience she knew that watercolors were always a hit, as were projects for their adored grandfather. The children happily moved on to the new activity, their cooperative spirit restored for the time being.

Another surprise move is the tickle attack. It's especially useful with younger children, but it can even be effective with teens. The tickler needs to be careful not to abuse the tickling and to stop when the child asks.

> The purple balloon that Kate, six, got at the doctor's was shriveled and due for the trash can. But her big brother, Brian, eleven, saw one last use for it. By exaggerating his interest in it, he could make Kate furious. He began to bounce it from hand to hand in front of her nose, hiding it under his shirt, and in general making it look like the best toy ever invented. Kate was just escalating from whining to screeching when Charlie, the Dad Tickle Monster, appeared in the nick of time yelling, "Tickle Attack!" Both kids dissolved in peals of laughter, and Charlie got a quick predinner workout. The balloon was completely forgotten and was quietly retired to the garbage can.

WHEN TO USE SURPRISE

Distracting is particularly effective with younger children, whose attention is easily diverted from a developing conflict. In addition, much of the boundary challenging that is typical of two-year-olds and four-year-olds can be happily diverted. The danger of surprise, as with other avoiding strategies, is that the real issue may not be addressed. If Brian's tormenting of his sister is becoming a regular event, the Tickle Monster may need to retire and other motives for sibling squabbles may need to be examined. Perhaps Brian is expressing a need for attention or limits, or perhaps Kate needs to learn to avoid setting herself up as a victim. As children get older, they tend to get wise to distracting strategies, and unless the alternative offered is very appealing, they may refuse to be sidetracked.

Often surprise strategies can turn a tense situation into an opportunity to have fun together. If your family tends to be serious or perfectionistic, both surprise and humor can lighten the mood at home. In addition children learn firsthand the value of playfulness in human interaction.

HUMOR

Humor is an effective form of distraction because it defuses the tension around the conflict. Often this is enough to dissolve the difficulty entirely, or it may help the people involved move to more effective problem solving or compromise. Humor can lighten up the often tumultuous interactions between adolescents and their parents.

Try changing roles at dinner, with each member pretending to be someone else. This gives you an opportunity to role-play other family members' table manners in a humorous way. Be prepared to see yourself from a new perspective when your kids lampoon your quirks. Be sure to keep it playful and positive, not sarcastic or negative. Clever or silly notes also offer great opportunities for humor. Using notes, parents have humorously requested assistance for a variety of jobs: "No maid service provided," or "Hello. I am the firewood. I am tired of getting wet. I would like to be stacked."

WHEN TO USE HUMOR

There is an art to using humor: Know your audience, and know your own feelings. If you're not in touch with your anger, your humor may have a cruel twist. Humor should be directed *at the situation,* not at the person. Sarcastic or humiliating humor may only aggravate the problem you're trying to solve, which is a clue to the fact that you may be using it to cover your anger or to avoid a situation that needs to be confronted.

WHAT IS STRUCTURING THE ENVIRONMENT?

The simple act of moving people or things around is often enough to reduce conflict. When two children riding in the backseat of the car start punching each other, one can be moved to the front seat. If a blaring TV is disturbing family members who are trying to study, either the TV or the homework gang can be moved to another room.

WHEN TO STRUCTURE THE ENVIRONMENT

As with other avoiding strategies, moving things around may only be a temporary solution that distracts from a bigger issue. If big sister's block-building projects are constantly tumbling into little brother's drawing space on the floor next to her, perhaps brother needs a table or desk space where he can pursue his art undisturbed. However, big sister may be placing herself in a position to torment her brother because she is resentful that her artistic brother gets so much attention from her parents. Acknowledging those feelings and setting up a schedule for special time with Mom and Dad might help reduce conflicts in the future.

The strategy of structuring the environment is useful for children of all ages. As children get older, they can offer creative suggestions for doing this. Ideas for altering the environment will often emerge when the family brainstorms as part of the problem-solving process.

TIPS FOR USING AVOIDING STRATEGIES

As you explore the avoiding strategies outlined in this chapter, keep in mind a few pointers:

- **Avoiding strategies are most effectively used when time or circumstances prevent direct action.** These techniques can buy time when you're upset or rushed. If the situation needs to be addressed later, make a plan using different approaches, such as problem solving or using consequences.

- **Keep track of your emotional temperature.** If what you're doing isn't working or if your irritation is on the rise, switch to another choice before you blow up.

- **Avoiding may be useful when your child is attempting to engage you in a power struggle or is seeking attention.** It is particularly helpful in handling the "lawyer" child or the debater.

- **Resist overuse of avoiding strategies.** It's tempting to avoid addressing an issue in order to keep your image as a "nice guy" when in fact limits need to be set. Also, some children will use your tendency to avoid as a way of getting what they want. The classic example is the child who acts out when her parent is occupied with an important phone call and can't address the behavior. This kind of problem will continue to recur if the parent doesn't make a plan of action and follow through.

- **Be careful not to mistake ignoring for long-term emotional withdrawal.** Overuse of this approach may give the child a message that you don't care or that you're not emotionally available. If you feel unaware of what's going on in your child's life, and if you don't spend much time together, it's important to examine this possibility.

Practicing

1. Keep a mental list of each time you ignore a conflict or a negative behavior in a day. Do you feel comfortable with your use of this avoidance strategy? If you would like to be more direct, practice directing statements. If you would like to ignore more disturbances, explore what is keeping you from doing so.

2. Plan ahead to try a humor or surprise response in a situation you know will "push your button." Share the results with your partner or friend.

3. Explore structuring the environment as a practical strategy for resolving a frequent conflict. Find an opportunity this week to try it. Report to your partner.

4. Use an avoiding strategy to buy time. This may be useful when you are in a hurry or in a public situation where you are uncomfortable dealing directly with the problem. Later you can address the issue by applying consequences or by problem solving.

10
Collaboration: Solving Problems Together

"Problem solving has changed my life! I used to avoid disciplining my kids because I didn't want to be unfair, as my father was with me. I found myself playing peacemaker between my kids, without a clue about setting limits. It was a minor miracle to discover that I could take time to cool off and we could all solve problems together later. The fairness issue was resolved by including the kids in more decisions, and I was relieved of having to act as judge, jury, and executioner on the spot."

—*Susan*

AS THIS EXCERPT FROM HER JOURNAL INDICATES, SUSAN SPENT MOST OF her eleven parenting years accommodating or ignoring much of her children's unacceptable behavior in order to avoid "playing the heavy." Until she began to change her methods, she wasn't even aware of how tiring it was to carry the full burden of providing all the answers by herself. Susan's discovery is not uncommon to parents who try out problem solving. They begin to unravel the knots of overresponsibility that have kept them entangled in decision after decision.

WHAT IS THE PROBLEM-SOLVING PROCESS?

The problem-solving process places parents and kids on a team, working together to solve conflicts. This gives both parents and children experience in making decisions and in learning from their mistakes. When problem solving, children learn to identify and express their feelings, to generate solutions, and to consider the effect of their actions. Since collaborative problem solving requires parents to listen to kids' input, it's a helpful strategy for the **directing** parent. Collaboration also works well for **accommodating** or **avoiding** parents, who often feel at a loss because they lack a fair strategy for addressing troublesome issues.

Many parents discover that the problem solving can be used to resolve differences between themselves and to brainstorm ideas for how to deal with problems with their kids. More on this in Chapter 13.

WHEN NOT TO USE PROBLEM SOLVING

Problem solving isn't a perfect answer to every problem. For one thing using problem solving *every time* you have a conflict is tedious for everyone involved, because it is more time-consuming than other strategies.

In addition, overusing this strategy may give your children the message that you are unable to take a leadership role. Avoid the temptation to use problem solving in order to dodge setting limits. Also be careful about using the process too frequently to intervene in conflicts between children. You might be giving them the message that they're not capable of solving their own problems, or you might be getting hooked into giving too much attention to minor squabbles.

Because problem solving can be time-consuming, don't do it when you're in a hurry. Instead, cool off and try one of the other C.H.O.I.C.E.S., then work together to solve the problem after the heat of the moment has passed. This is especially important for issues that carry extra emotional weight. Wait for a calm moment or set a planned time to solve the problem. As described in Chapter 12, family meetings offer a practical setting for this process.

Be as clear as possible with both yourself and your kids about which decisions you are willing to share and which issues are non-negotiable. You may suddenly realize after half an hour of searching for solutions with your children that you are comfortable with only one idea: your own. Explain this to them honestly. Obviously it would have been far better for everyone involved, and less awkward for you, if you had used a directing strategy from the start. Sometimes during the problem-solving process we gain new understanding about the situation or about how we really feel. Collaboration is a learning process for parents and for children. Making mistakes together is part of learning together.

WHEN TO USE PROBLEM SOLVING

Children are usually able to begin participating in the problem-solving process around age four, although they won't be adept collaborators at this age. Problem solving is particularly effective as children move through ages where issues of power and independence are foremost, such as during adolescence. Problem solving is also a survival tool for the parent of a "power struggle" child. Giving this kind of child more power in making real decisions about her life seems to help reduce her need to prove her power in negative ways. The "lawyer" child can also be disarmed by use of this choice. If he shares in the decision, he is less likely to put his talent for debate into verbal sparring with his parents. If he later argues the results of the problem-solving process, a written copy serves as proof of the agreement. A very shy or quiet child may need encouragement to participate in problem solving. Kids who are hostile or who have an extremely hard time relating to other people will have difficulty with this process. These children may need the help of an outside professional.

SETTING THE PROBLEM-SOLVING PROCESS IN MOTION

Try to imagine how your children will perceive your first attempt at problem solving. The children of parents who are usually **directing** won't be easily persuaded that there is any intention to share parental authority. They may not buy into the process. Children of an **avoider** or **accommodator** may not believe that there is a real commitment to following through with whatever solution is reached. They will need to be convinced that you are serious about taking action.

If your conflict style falls strongly into one of these categories, sit down with your children and let them know you are approaching some of the problems that arise in the family in a different way. If your usual approach is directing, tell them that you intend to share some of the responsibility for decision making with them. If you have a history of poor follow-through, let them know that you're serious about sticking with any decisions you make together. It helps to start with a smaller item, such as what to plan for a family activity next week, and to have a plan in place for checking back.

PROBLEM SOLVING IN ACTION

Cliff dashed into the bathroom to finish getting ready before catching his car pool to work. "Where's my brush?" he bellowed. This was not the first time his brush had "walked away" from the bathroom, and Cliff's frustration was mounting. He stepped out into the hallway and shouted, "Who used my brush?" A wall of silence greeted him. Glowering, he rummaged through the bathroom drawers until he found an old beat-up comb. He quickly ran it through his hair and was out the door, barely in time to catch his ride. On the way home that day Cliff thought about what had happened that morning and decided he needed to do something to eliminate the daily hairbrush hassles. At dinner that night he broached the subject with his wife and two daughters, ages six and eleven.

"I feel really frustrated because lately my brush has been disappearing from the bathroom. When I'm rushed in the morning, it drives me nuts not to be able to find what I need. Anybody have any ideas about what's been happening?'"

Cliff's wife, Sherry, grinned at him guiltily. "Becky and I use your brush when I'm braiding her hair in the morning, and I guess we've been forgetting to put it back when we're done,"

"Why can't you use her brush?" Cliff replied.

Becky piped up, "I don't have my own, and all the others aren't soft enough. Yours is the only one that feels good."

After a little more conversation Cliff summed up the problem. "So the problem seems to be that my brush keeps disappearing from the bathroom because you two are using it and forgetting to put it back. I want my brush to stay in the bathroom, and Becky wants to use my brush because it is the only one that feels good to her. Let's brainstorm some ideas to solve this problem. Remember, anything goes, and we don't make fun of other people's ideas."

They came up with the following list:

- Shave off Cliff's hair

- Buy a different brush for each person in the family

- Cliff could buy a new brush of his own

- Cliff could use any brush he found

- Cliff could wear his hair shorter

- Everyone could give Cliff a dollar when his brush was missing

- The girls could pay a dollar when the brush was missing

- Forget about the whole thing

After they were finished brainstorming, Cliff said, "Let's evaluate our ideas. What might happen if I shave off my hair?"

"Your head might get cold," his daughter Mandy suggested.

"You might lose your job because you look funny," his wife teased.

"I guess that idea won't work. Let's cross it off the list," Cliff said.

They continued down the list until several were eliminated. During the planning that followed, the family decided that each person should have his or her own brush. This involved purchasing a smaller brush like Dad's for Becky. Other brushes that the family already owned were divvied up among the rest of the clan. They agreed that the brushes would be stored in a designated container in the bathroom and that each person would be responsible for keeping track of his or her own. They would check back in a week to see how their plan was working.

The following week Cliff brought up the issue for review, and the whole family agreed that it had been a success. A transgression still occurs now and then, but on the whole Cliff feels they made considerable progress on the issue.

THE PROBLEM-SOLVING PROCESS IN BRIEF

Let's see how Cliff and his family applied the basic steps of problem solving to resolve the hairbrush conflict.

1. Gather Information
Give everyone a chance to tell what happened, how they are feeling, and what they want. Cliff started the family discussion by sharing how he was feeling and what was making him feel that way. Then he invited the rest of the family to share their points of view. "I feel really frustrated because lately my brush has been disappearing from the bathroom. When I'm rushed in the morning, it drives me nuts not to be able to find it. I want to be able to find it when I need it. Anybody have any ideas about what's been happening?"
2. Define the Problem
Summarize the problem clearly, expressing what each person wants. "So the problem seems to be that my brush keeps disappearing from the bathroom because you two are using it and forgetting to put it back. I want my brush to stay in the bathroom, and Becky wants to use my brush because it is the only one that feels good to her."
3. Generate Ideas
Brainstorm many ideas, both crazy and practical, that might solve the problem, and write them all down. "Now let's brainstorm some ideas. Remember, anything goes, and we don't make fun of other people's ideas."
4. Evaluate
Look at the consequences of each idea. "Let's evaluate our ideas. What might happen if I shave off my hair?"
5. Make a Plan
Choose one or more ideas from your brainstormed list and make a plan. Check back within a week to see how it's working.
Cliff, Sherry, and the kids expanded and revised two ideas from their list to come up with a solution, and they scheduled a check back for the next weekend.

A CLOSER LOOK AT PROBLEM SOLVING

In our classes we find that as parents become more familiar with the problem-solving process, it is helpful to get more detailed information about the steps of the process. The ideas and insights below will help you and your family refine your problem-solving skills.

STEPS 1 AND 2: GATHERING INFORMATION AND DEFINING THE PROBLEM

Good communication skills are the key to understanding all points of view and clarifying what the real problem is. Listen carefully as you gather information, and avoid blaming or name-calling as each person describes his or her experiences and needs. We'll provide more ideas on communication at the end of the chapter.

Often we jump to conclusions and go after the symptom rather than the cause of the problem. Carefully gathering information helps us to find and clarify the real problem.

> Neal was angry with his son, John, who missed the bus home from school several days in a row. They lived so far from school that this meant that Neal had to leave work early or make spur-of-the-moment arrangements with a friend or neighbor to pick up his son. After some angry interchanges during which Neal accused his son of missing the bus because of goofing around in the halls, they tried a problem-solving session. As it turned out, John was avoiding leaving the classroom until the very last minute because he was being teased by older kids while he waited for the bus. Armed with this new information, they brainstormed some solutions to the real problem. They decided that, for the time being, John could use another bus that stopped three blocks from their house, or he could walk to a city bus stop. In addition they agreed that John would talk to the school counselor, who might be able to help John figure out how to handle the teasing. Neal also placed a call to the building principal to see what could be done about supervising the children while they waited for their bus.

You should continue gathering information throughout the problem-solving process. New insights into the problem may come up in brainstorming, evaluating, or even while you're developing a plan.

As you define the problem, it's extremely important to clarify each person's positions and interests. A *position* is *what* a person wants. An *interest* is *why* the person wants it. Separating positions and interests often helps define the problem and move the process forward. Roger Fisher, author of *Getting to Yes,* a classic in conflict resolution, tells a story that illustrates this point. Two sisters were in a heated battle over the last orange in the kitchen. Their mother immediately attempted to solve the problem by cutting it in half and dividing it between the girls. They still weren't satisfied. One sister had wanted the peel of an orange to make a cake; the other wanted to eat the orange. If they had first discussed why they wanted the orange (their interests), both girls could have met their needs. Since they stayed stuck on what they wanted (their positions), they were unable to resolve their differences.

Jeanne's ten-year-old son, Andy, was having difficulty remembering to do his daily chores and asked to trade these smaller chores for doing the family laundry on the weekends, along with a boost in his allowance. This seemed like a big responsibility for a ten-year-old, and Jeanne and John were skeptical about whether he could handle it. Their standards were fairly relaxed about doing laundry anyway, and he seem highly motivated, so they decided to try it. To live with the plan, however, Jeanne knew she'd have to take care of the fine washables herself. Andy's job included folding and delivering clothes to their owners' rooms. For two weekends John trained Andy in the various tasks he would need as the family laundry expert, from operating the machine to sorting and folding. The family launderer did a great job for two months, with occasional prompting. Then things started to slide. The laundry was washed and dried, but it was left in huge mounds beside the machines.

After a few Monday mornings in a row without clean underwear in her drawer, Jeanne was fed up. She announced that it was time for Andy to find a new job. Later the whole family discussed the situation at a family meeting. Their conversation revealed that Andy loved the laundering part of the laundry job, but he didn't like the folding and putting-away part of it. He wanted to continue doing just the laundry. Jeanne's *position* was that Andy should have a different job. Her *interest* (why she demanded that Andy switch jobs) was that she wanted to have clean laundry put away before the hectic week started Monday morning. Once she was able to separate her position from her interest, they were able to work out an agreement in which both their needs were met. Andy continued doing the first part of the laundry job, and Jeanne and John took over the folding and delivery.

STEP 3: BRAINSTORMING

When you first begin problem solving, you may find yourself stuck for ideas as you brainstorm. Rest assured that the more you do it, the easier it will get. To ease your initial discomfort, use the list of "C.H.O.I.C.E.S. for Managing Conflict" in Chapter 6 to come up with some solutions that feel comfortable to you. Allow plenty of time for your children to generate ideas when you're problem solving together. Throwing out crazy suggestions makes the process much more fun. Write down *all* the ideas, no matter how silly. Even the most absurd idea may contain the kernel of an original solution.

Bouts of punching and kicking between siblings were beginning to escalate in the Copeland household as the summer wore on. Mary and Ted gathered their three children together, sat them down, and asked for suggestions on how to stop the negative behavior. They accepted all ideas:

- Put the kids in jail

- Kids go to separate rooms to cool off

- Fight with words, not fists

- Ask grown-ups for help

- Kill each other

- Find somebody else to fight with

- Mother or Daddy stop doing dishes and help settle it

- Parents pretend to be the kids, and kids pretend to be the parents

- Parents assign other things to do to people who fight

- Kids decide on something else to do

- Train kids to not fight; teach us to solve problems

- Get a punching bag

- Have celebration cake if there's no fighting for two weeks

- Make a rule that if we don't stop fighting, we can't play together for rest of the day

As their list indicates, the Copelands were experienced and inventive brainstormers. The range of solutions, from practical to absurd, offers a variety of options. They'd learned to allow some time in between ideas and to wait for the creative bursts that sometimes follow a brief silence. Once they were satisfied that they had generated enough ideas, they were ready to move on to evaluating them.

STEPS 4 AND 5: EVALUATING AND MAKING A PLAN

Evaluating brainstorms and making a plan can be just as creative as the rest of the process. Putting the kids in jail or killing each other might seem a little drastic to the serious parent. However, the family discussed creating a pretend jail as a humorous solution. By ushering kids to a pretend jail, they would be reminded of the issue, while humor dissolved the tension around the fight. As it was, however, a celebration cake was the family's favored solution, and it worked. Bringing the issue to everyone's attention and celebrating success were enough to resolve the problem, at least for the rest of the summer vacation.

One good evaluation strategy is to ask, "What might happen if we do that?" Children of all ages need practice in considering the possible consequences of their choices. Some families use the Three *R*s of consequences, described in Chapter 5, to guide them in evaluating their brainstorms. For example, the Copelands looked at each item and asked themselves if it was reasonable, respectful, and related to the problem. When they'd finished, several ideas were still left on the list, but they were most excited about trying the celebration-cake choice.

Once the plan is made, the first few days of follow-through are essential. It takes an initial time commitment before any new policy becomes second nature. Many a great plan has been lost in the aftermath if other priorities crowd it out. Use family meetings to check on the new plan, and if it's not working, check the brainstormed list and try a different approach.

Sometimes you don't need to follow the process all the way to the final steps of evaluating and making a plan. Talking about the problem and tossing around some ideas may be enough.

> Stuart was concerned about the amount of food wasted in his household. He found bowls full of soggy cereal left in the sink, and he was continually scraping uneaten food off his kids' plates after dinner. He aired his concerns, and the family brainstormed a list of solutions: allowing all of them to serve themselves, each person eating all the food he or she chooses, and putting leftovers into the refrigerator more quickly, among others. After they'd talked about it, the family agreed that they needed to be more careful about wasting food, but they decided that they'd just try to remind each other to be more careful for the time being. No decision was made in favor of any one solution, but the problem took care of itself.

SKILLFUL LISTENING AND SHARING CAN ENHANCE PROBLEM SOLVING

Many conflicts are caused by misunderstanding the other person's intentions or actions. Sensitivity to others' points of view and an ability to express one's own without fanning the flames of the conflict are fundamental to the problem-solving process. Being a capable communicator means knowing how to listen attentively and how to state one's feelings clearly.

ATTENTIVE LISTENING

When we listen attentively, the other person feels understood and valued. When we don't feel understood and valued, we tend to get caught up in defending ourselves and our position, and we're unwilling to work toward a mutually satisfying solution. In addition, knowing more about the other person helps us come up with solutions that satisfy his or her needs.

Attentive listening, adapted from active listening, a key concept in Parent Effectiveness Training, developed by Thomas Gordon, includes these basic elements:

• **Give nonverbal signals that show that you're all ears** (including eye contact and attentive posture and facial expressions).

- **Encourage your children to elaborate on their thinking** by nodding, making neutral comments ("Hmmm . . . " or "Uh-huh . . . "), and by asking leading questions ("Tell me more about that," or "How did you feel about that?").

- **Show that you understand what is being said by rephrasing the main content occasionally** ("So you would like your friends to ask you before they take things from your desk, right?"). Avoid giving advice or making suggestions.

- **Reflect to the speaker the feeling that underlies what is being shared** ("It really made you mad when they took your favorite pencil from your desk," or "You seem frustrated with Jenny."). This process helps children to clarify their feelings and also serves as a good way to check your understanding of what has been said.

If you listen closely and ask questions that help your children sort out their thinking, you can often uncover unmet needs or hidden aspects of the issue. Recently Susan's ten-year-old daughter, Johanna, came home from the swimming pool in tears about the way her friends had treated her. Susan suggested they sit on the porch swing and talk about it.

"When Stephanie called just before noon, she asked me to meet her at the pool right away. But when I got there, she started playing with Marta and Kerry and then started acting so silly. When I started acting silly, too, Marta told me, 'Johanna, you're so stupid when you do that.' I was just acting like Stephanie acted, and they thought *she* was funny."

"It's really hard when kids you want to be with treat you that way, isn't it?" Susan asked.

"Yes, and every kid I know does that to me sometimes," she answered.

"Sounds like you're feeling pretty hurt. What did you do today when they acted mean?" Susan continued to ask for information, hoping to clarify the problem.

"I just went and played Marco Polo with some other kids. If they want to be that way, let them," Johanna responded.

"Was it fun?"

"Yeah. I had a good time. I saw Lizzie. She was nice to me, but she's always with someone else too. She goes there every day. I hate going to that pool," she went on, starting to tear up again.

"It sounds like you took good care of yourself by finding something else to do, but you still seem upset. I'm wondering why that might be," Susan said.

"It's just that I don't have anyone to count on that I can just relax and have fun with. The only one is Rachel, and now she's always with Heather." Johanna began to sob.

"Ah, honey. It's really hard to share such a good friend, I know." Susan put her arm around Johanna while she cried. "Maybe you can think of someone you'd like to play with tomorrow here, to get a break from the scene at the pool. How about Bryn? She called the other day."

"That's a good idea," Johanna said, but she continued to cry. "I don't feel too good. My head feels funny."

Susan held her for a minute, then she asked, "When did you last eat?"

"Well, I dunno. I ate some toast and a banana this morning." Susan looked at her watch. It was five-thirty.

Susan had used her best listening skills, carefully searching for underlying issues and problems. She concluded that Johanna was feeling vulnerable and was missing an old pal and that she might need some support to set up play dates with new friends. By listening harder, however, she also discovered that her child's hunger was magnifying her emotional response and lowering her ability to bounce back. Friendship problems could be more easily addressed once she'd eaten.

Allow plenty of time for effective listening. The extra effort may save time in the long run, and it's a great investment in developing family rapport.

FEELING STATEMENTS

Often we bring strong emotions to the problem-solving process. Feeling statements (adapted from the classic "I Message," developed by Thomas Gordon in Parent Effectiveness Training) give us a way to express our feelings without aggravating the situation, since they help us avoid blaming and name-calling. A formula for feeling statements might look like this: "**I feel [state your feeling] when [describe the specific behavior].**"

Another variation on feeling statements gives more information: "**I feel [state your feeling] when [describe the specific behavior] because [the effect of the behavior on you].**" Psychologist

H. Stephen Glenn suggests that this gives the child valuable feedback about why his or her behavior has the effect that it does on
us. "I feel frustrated when dirty clothes and wet towels are left in
the bathroom because then I have to clean up before I can take
my shower." Knowing this, the child can generalize about how the
same behavior might affect others or how a similar behavior might
affect you under other circumstances. This also opens the way for
discussion, which can lead to problem solving.

Pair a feeling statement with a simple directive: "I'm feeling frustrated that you didn't start your chores when I asked you, and I
want you to start them now." This adds a new twist to the command strategy. Like other commands this may require follow-
through.

The hardest thing about this kind of message is remembering to
use it, according to Gail Sadalla, international conflict-resolution
trainer. This is because we're often angry when we need to be
using feeling statements, and when we're mad, it's hard to slow
down and express ourselves carefully. Problem solving gives us an
excellent opportunity to practice feeling statements, since we're
more likely to be focused on resolving the issue than on being
angry about it.

TIPS FOR USING COLLABORATION

- **Acknowledge anger.** Use feeling statements in the information-
gathering phase to help dissipate angry feelings. After doing this,
take time to cool off if anyone is too angry to proceed constructively with the problem-solving process.

- **While brainstorming, you may need to continue restating
the problem to keep your problem solvers focused on the
issue.** This is especially true with younger children.

- **Stay focused on seeking solutions rather than on blaming.**
If your problem solvers are getting sidetracked into blaming or
name-calling, say, "Let's try looking for a solution rather than
blaming."

- **On bigger issues write down your agreement and have your
kids sign it,** especially if you have a child who may later try to
argue you out of the terms of the solution.

- **If your children refuse to cooperate in the problem-solving
process, you can offer a choice:** Either they can help with

solving the problem or you, as the parent, will make the decision.

- **Affirm your children as peacemakers and problem solvers.** After your children have some experience with problem solving, give them a vote a confidence: "I'm sure you two can work that out. You're good problem solvers." Point it out to your children when they successfully solve problems.

Judicious use of problem solving, combined with the other C.H.O.I.C.E.S., provides all the tools you need for creative conflict resolution.

Problem Solving with Your Child

(First ask yourself: Is cooling off necessary before you proceed with problem solving?)

1. Get your child's attention by stating the problem as you see it.
Use a feeling statement to share how you experienced the situation. Avoid blaming.

"I feel _____ when _____."

2. Gather information.
Invite your child to share his or her point of view. Use feeling statements and attentive listening.

"Is there something I need to know that will help me understand how you see the situation?"
"What happened?"
"How did you feel when _____?"
"Tell me more about that."

Discuss the problem together.

"I felt _____ when _____. How did you feel?"
"Tell me more about that."
"How did you feel when _____?"

3. State the problem.

State the problem so it expresses everyone's needs:

> *"You want _____, and I want _____. What can we do so everyone will be happy?"* or *"What can we do to meet everyone's needs?"*

4. Generate ideas.

Encourage lots of ideas, both crazy and practical. Accept all ideas without criticism.

> *"Let's see how many ideas we can think of to solve this problem."*
> *"Remember that anything goes, no matter how crazy, and we don't criticize any ideas when we're brainstorming."*

Write down all ideas.
You may need to remind kids what the problem is by restating it frequently.

> *"Remember, the problem we're working on is _____."*

5. Evaluate.

Look at the consequences of each idea.

> *"What might happen if we (state idea)?"*
> *"Would that make both people happy?"* or *"How can we meet everyone's needs?"*
> *"Is it reasonable, respectful, and related?"*

6. Make a plan.

Use one or more of the brainstorm ideas to make a plan.

> *"The idea of _____ seems to be one that everyone likes. Shall we try it?"*

If you're having trouble reaching an agreement, say,

> *"Would you be willing to try _____ for a week?"*

Make a plan to evaluate the decision later with your child and decide together if it was successful.

"Let's talk about how our plan is working next week at _____."

If it wasn't successful, plan for more problem solving, if appropriate.

"It seems like our solution didn't work out very well. Let's see if we can figure out why and then change it so it will work better next time."

If it was successful, congratulate yourselves on your problem solving.

"We really did a good job coming up with a solution for the _____ problem."

Practicing

1. Recall a recent conflict at home or work. Describe your position and interest and try to identify the position and interest of the other person involved.

2. Before problem solving with your child practice the process on a small problem. Write down your brainstorms or go through the process aloud with a friend. Use the problem-solving guide on the preceding page.

3. Practice attentive listening with your child. Set aside ten minutes to give him or her your total attention, following the guidelines described in this chapter.

4. With older children take turns practicing attentive listening. Ask each person to take a one-minute turn sharing something special they did in the last few days. Talk about how this felt.

5. Think of feeling statements for the following situations:

• You're ticked off because your teenage son and his friend polished off a quart of your special diet yogurt.

• You're trying to balance your checkbook and your kids keep interrupting you with a disagreement they're having over a board game.

• Your eleven-year-old comes home an hour late for dinner.

6. Think of a situation with your child that might occur in the next few days in which you might use a feeling statement. Imagine what you'll say and how your child will respond. Share this with your friend or spouse. Then try it.

PART THREE

From Conflict to Cooperation: Building a Caring Climate

"The greenhouse structure creates a climate that is a safe haven for tender plants to grow and bloom."
—Paul, Flowerland Nursery

11
Mad Kids: What's a Parent to Do?

*"Tom, Rob, and I were playing a basketball game and we were doing fine until Tom challenged me! I was champ at the time so I had to 'fight' him. All went well until the end, when I thought Tom was doing something that was agenst the rules of the game. Of course I was beatan (because of the 'cheating'). Then I complained to Rob but every time I said something to him he'd say something like 'I didn't see it.' Then I'd say, 'But you were standing right there! You are a bad ref.' Every time I commplined it seems like he would ignore me more than the time before. Then I 'blew my stack.' At the time that it happened I was realy mad, but after a week or two I can laugh at my foolishness! The main problem in this insadint was the not listening to others. I admet that I didn't listen and I'm sorry I got in a fight at all! Tom and Rob didn't even look at me and if they did they did it very little I hated that because Tom invited Rob over when I was already there (he does it all the time, the only friend I like him to do this with is Zach). I know I handled my anger wrong. I'd like to keep working on leving when my anger escalates to that point. **I'm sorry Rob!**"*

—*Luke, age eleven*

THIS DESCRIPTION OF A FIGHT WAS WRITTEN WITH INVENTIVE SPELLING by eleven-year-old Luke, with little adult prompting. For him, as for most children, anger is an intense and overwhelming emotion. He struggles with his anger at being treated unfairly and at not being heard. As he describes what happened when he blew up at Tom and Rob, Luke reveals surprising understanding of himself and of the causes of his anger. He describes the problems and how he'd like to change his behavior. He's also able to look at what needs changing in the situation itself so that the problem isn't as likely to repeat itself.

Luke is learning to manage his anger by understanding his anger cycle and by making a plan for those behaviors he can change. As a result "I can handle this!" will be his self-talk concerning his anger as he moves into adulthood.

RESPONDING TO YOUR CHILD'S ANGER

Anger can be a very scary emotion, especially to a young child. We can help our children manage these fears in three ways:

• **Naming** the feeling

• **Acknowledging** and **accepting** anger

• Helping the child **channel** it appropriately

When children are very young, we can help them manage their anger by giving them words to describe their feelings: "You seem to be feeling really angry about this." Naming and accepting angry feelings are the first steps toward self-control.

The next step is to help them find appropriate ways to channel feelings. Physical outlets for aggressive feelings are sometimes helpful to all of us. In the long run, however, we want to do more than teach children to release their aggression. We want them to learn to separate the angry feeling from the action, to know that they can choose how to act in response to their anger, and to be responsible for the action they choose.

It's tempting to respond to children's anger with punishment. However, this not only tells them that the angry feeling isn't okay, but it may also escalate the anger. The focus of anger then shifts to you for having punished them. This distracts children from looking at their own choice in their behavior and the consequences of that choice.

A reasonable consequence, directed not at the anger itself but at the mischanneling of it, focuses children on taking responsibility for the action they've chosen. It also helps children resolve residual bad feelings about losing control of themselves. It may help to memorize a script beforehand: "I can see that you are angry, but it is not okay to break your sister's toy." Plan ahead how you will follow up on your lines, such as moving the child to another location to cool off (**direct action**) or requiring that the broken item be replaced (**consequence**).

HELPING KIDS MAKE EFFECTIVE CHOICES IN THE ANGER CYCLE

Children move through the same anger cycle that adults do, and they need similar coping strategies. Coupled with problem-solving skills, these strategies can move them toward constructive solutions that will be helpful on the sports field, on the playground, in the neighborhood, and at home.

PRE-ANGER APPROACHES

One mistake we make as adults is to assume that children should handle their anger in an adult manner. Managing anger involves self-awareness and self-control. It involves separating the feeling itself from the action that expresses it. It means making choices on how to act on the anger and then weighing up the good and bad consequences of those choices.

For younger children, learning to head off anger is a very complex task, which begins with learning to recognize and name the feeling. Children as young as four can brainstorm cooling-off strategies ("What could you do to help yourself feel better?") but will have difficulty initiating these when they're angry. A supportive adult can offer firm but kind guidance by saying, "I see that you are angry. You need to find something to do in your room to help yourself feel better, and later we'll talk about what happened." The child may need to be gently but firmly escorted to the designated cooling-off area. Because angry feelings are frightening to young children, they need the reassurance that everybody gets angry, that anger won't hurt others, and that you will help them learn to control angry impulses.

Older children can learn to recognize times of the day or stressful situations when they are likely to be vulnerable to their anger. As a parent you can comment on your child's pattern: "This is one of those situations where I've noticed you're likely to get angry. Is there something you can do to take care of yourself if you start to feel stressed or upset?" These questions might help the child become conscious of her own anger patterns. Some parents and kids agree on a hand signal to use at such times.

Another way to head off anger before it gets going is to talk about it at calmer times. Brainstorming a list of anger-producing situations with your children can yield useful insights. For instance here's the list Andy gave us when he was eleven:

• Losing a game

• Not taking turns in an agreeable way

• Doing something and getting in trouble when someone else who did the same thing doesn't get in trouble

• When I'm really hungry

• When someone else throws the first punch (physically or emotionally)

• When someone works on something I want to work on alone

• When someone interrupts something important

• When someone cheats, tries to cheat, or does something that looks like cheating

• When someone says something wrong about me

• Lots of stress

• Headaches

WHAT TO DO BEFORE THE BOIL-OVER

As children become more adept at labeling, they can learn to differentiate between the "little anger" of frustration and the "big anger" of rage. This understanding will be helpful as they choose which strategies will work for diverting the anger.

Next help them find acceptable actions to channel their angry feelings. Encourage a younger child to express his or her feelings by suggesting, "Use your words." Feed the words to an angry child who is struggling with this. "Tell Katie, 'I don't like it when you take my toy.' " While the eventual goal is to move toward talking about the cause of the anger and solving the problem, some younger children may need physical outlets for rechanneling anger. Punching a pillow or mattress, tearing up old newspapers, drawing a "mad scribble" picture, or hammering on toys that are constructed for pounding will release angry energy harmlessly.

As children move into middle childhood, rehearsing anger-management techniques is helpful. Discuss the child's handling of anger and review what has worked well for him in the past, as well as what hasn't worked so well. Teach him to use self-talk (such as, *I can handle this without losing my cool*) when he's starting to heat up. A hand signal can be effective in helping your child tune in to his feelings or to suggest that he take action to cool off. It's also useful to give children examples of phrases they can use to get out of an anger-producing situation: "I'm too mad to talk about this now. I'm going home."

Brainstorm a list of things to do when the temperature begins to rise. Three thirteen-year-old boys generated the following list:

• Play video games and get revenge on characters

• Put on headphones and listen to favorite music

• Draw a picture of the person you're mad at

• Eat—you could have a short fuse because you're hungry

• Write a story with the person you're mad at as the main character

• Slam doors when no one is around

• Run laps around the house

• Cool off in your room

• Work on homework

• Practice a sport

• Pretend you're flying to Mars or swimming to Hawaii

Other children have found it helps to get something to drink, to count to ten backward, to go to a favorite outdoor hideout, or to talk it out with a friend or grown-up.

When children verbally express their angry feelings toward other kids, there is always the possibility that other children will respond by ignoring them or by saying, "So what?" Kids need ideas about what to do if using words doesn't help. Our adolescent assistants generated this unique list:

• Walk away

• Swear and punch them

• Calm down

• Get help

• Ignore them and go on with what you were doing

• Figure out a way to outsmart them and get what you want

• Tell them to bug off

Remember, brainstorming works best, and it's more fun, if you accept all solutions as they come up. Obviously some of these brainstorm ideas would prove inappropriate if we asked, "What might happen if I do that?" However, several of the solutions do have practical value.

BOILING-OVER STRATEGIES

Once the boiling point is reached, attempts at intervening verbally usually result in making the child angrier. As long as the situation is reasonably safe, the child needs cooling-down time. Some children are comforted by being gently hugged by a parent. Others need to be left alone. After the angry feelings begin to fade, you can suggest that the child do something to make herself feel better.

AFTER THE BOIL-OVER: WHAT TO DO

First of all, make sure your child is really cooled off before you do anything. Help your child reflect on what happened and begin to put together a plan for handling the next heated situation. Questions to guide you might include:

• What happened?

• Why did it happen?

• What was it like for you?

• What could you do next time so that things might go differently?

According to psychologists H. Stephen Glenn and Jane Nelsen, in their book *Raising Self-Reliant Children in a Self-Indulgent World*, asking these questions is crucial in guiding children to understand and channel their anger appropriately: "Children develop self-control when they see the relationship between feelings and actions, actions and outcomes. The goal here is for them to understand, 'I feel _____, I do _____, I experience _____. Next time I *feel* a certain emotion, I might *do* something different so I can *experience* another outcome.' " It is important to practice this kind of thinking over and over with children to help them learn to manage this complex emotion.

TEMPER TANTRUMS

Expect your child to have temper tantrums between the ages of two and four. This is a normal behavior for this developmental stage. Respond with love and concern, but don't cave in to the child's wish or get overinvolved with his feelings. Try to stay calm, remembering to use self-talk.

> One parent of a two-and-a-half-year-old was completely exasperated by her child's continual outbursts. She tried everything, from spankings to bribery. When she shared this in our parenting class, a knowing chuckle went around the group. Most people there had war stories to share from their experience with a two-year-old. They offered strategies that helped them survive this predictable stage: leaving the scene, physically removing the child so that he could cool off, helping the child to calm down by rocking or hugging him. By listening to other parents, this mother began to see her child's behavior as normal, and she also gathered some specific ideas to move through this challenging time in child rearing.

Older children will also occasionally throw a temper tantrum. Encourage them to cool off and to come back when they are ready to discuss the problem. After the tantrum discuss what happened, using the questions suggested for use after boiling over. If tantrums become a pattern, however, look a little deeper. Is the child using the tantrum to manipulate? If so, try out one of the C.H.O.I.C.E.S. for guiding behavior. A **commanding** strategy might be helpful. Give the child a clear message about what behavior is expected: "You need to get in control now. You can choose to act differently."

Do the temper tantrums occur in a specific situation or with a specific person? Consider what's happening in that situation and what strategies or consequences will be most likely to work. Sometimes the child's behavior is a reflection of an unmet need. Explore this possibility, but avoid making too many allowances for the child's behavior. The unmet need may be to know the limits or to find out what behavior will be tolerated by adults. You're doing your child a favor by helping him change a behavior that will, in the long run, damage his relationships with others.

TEMPERAMENTAL ISSUES

Some kids are inclined by temperament to have a shorter fuse. For these kids it is even more important for parents to provide firm guidance and consistent practice. Use the information from this chapter to guide you in making a plan to support this child. Celebrate small improvements and remember past triumphs when you're feeling discouraged.

As a parent, you've probably observed situations that typically lead to episodes of anger. For some children overstimulation is likely to result in an outburst of anger. For others the strain of a new encounter is enough to trigger a tirade. A little detective work may pay off here. Look at what you can do to **structure the situation** to minimize the likelihood of trouble. One mother discovered that her son was easily overwhelmed in new situations and acted this out by behaving aggressively toward other children. She found that taking him to a new place before others arrived helped him adjust, and she kept these potentially stressful experiences to a minimum.

THE PARENT IN THE MIRROR

It's okay for your kids to see you get mad. If our children don't see us manage our own anger, they may get the message that it's bad to have angry feelings. They'll also be robbed of role models for handling anger in healthy ways. If they learn to deny it, anger will emerge as depression, revenge, rebellion, or will build into uncontrollable outbursts.

If you don't handle your anger well, you always have the opportunity to model how to recover. "I made a mistake. . . . I apologize. . . . Let's work on a solution together." It's never too late to admit your mistake and to apologize or to make a plan to change the circumstances that led to the outburst. This is effective with individual family members as well as with the entire group.

One strategy for teaching kids about anger is to share your own difficulties managing your cooling system, asking them for ideas on how you might be more effective at handling it. As your children brainstorm with you, they are indirectly gaining insights into handling their own anger.

The communication skills we model will also build the strong foundation necessary for kids to deal with their own anger. Children who have heard their parents use feeling statements and attentive listening will be less likely to vent their anger inappropriately.

> Suzanne frequently blew off steam by yelling or stomping around the house, slamming doors. She was disturbed when she saw her five-year-old daughter mirroring this behavior, and she began to take a look at the lessons she'd taught with her own actions. When Suzanne brought the issue to parenting class, she brainstormed with the group some ways she could change her behavior. The class helped her make a plan.
>
> The next few times she felt her patience waning, Suzanne indicated this by making a clear statement: "I have this much patience left," holding up her fingers to indicate a pinch. After that she focused on doing something to calm herself down so that the situation wouldn't escalate.
>
> A few weeks later her daughter was exasperated with her dad for not responding to the fifth request that he listen to her. From the next room the mother overheard her daughter's high voice, "I have this much patience left with you."

Keep the goal of anger management in mind, but remember that you're working with your child on a complex change. Anger control is difficult for most adults. Recognize and celebrate little achievements along the way. Stay with it. It's only when a child is old enough to think more abstractly that she can generalize about the effect of her actions on others and can develop true empathy.

TIPS FOR MANAGING ANGER

- **Sometimes a child's pattern of angry outbursts and physical aggression are expressions of a need for more limits.** Renew your commitment to set limits and make a plan to do so using C.H.O.I.C.E.S. and follow-through strategies.

- **Remember that your child's behavior may get worse before it starts to improve.** Some parents find that family counseling helps to bring a particularly difficult situation back within healthy bounds.

- **Notice when your anger gets in the way of dealing effectively with your child's anger.** Use self-talk and cooling-off strategies, and buy time.

- **Avoid problem solving until everyone is cooled off.**

- **Family meetings provide a forum for discussion and problem solving after the air has cleared.**

- **If your child has a regular pattern of angry outbursts, check to see if she is using it to manipulate you and/or others or is expressing an unmet need.** Refer to Chapters 4 and 6 for help.

Practicing

1. How would you describe your style of managing anger? How is it similar to or different from your parents'? How is it similar to or different from your child's? Share this with your spouse or a friend.

2. Talk to your family about how you manage your own anger and ask them how you might be more effective in handling it. Practice your listening skills as they give you feedback.

3. If you have a younger child, look for opportunities to teach him to name, acknowledge, accept, and channel his anger. With your partner or a friend, brainstorm creative ideas. One suggestion: The next time your child is angry at you or a sibling, give him crayons and paper and have him draw how angry he is.

4. Think about how you might respond differently the next time your child has an angry outburst. Relax, close your eyes, and envision in detail what you will do the next time your child gets angry. Tell your parenting partner or friend about your plan.

5. Brainstorm with your child a list of cooling-off strategies that work for her.

6. The next time you notice your child getting angry with a friend, discuss what you saw and ask your child to think of self-talk to help him keep his cool next time. "I wonder what you could say to yourself, using the voice inside you, to keep it from getting to you."

7. With your child or a small group of kids, brainstorm a list of ways to respond when another child is being aggravating. Then go over the list and ask, "What might happen if you do this?" for each idea.

8. With your child, role-play new responses to situations in which he usually loses control. Talk about the situation first: "Who is involved?" "What exactly did they do or say?" "How were you feeling?" "How were they feeling?" "What are some other ways to respond?" You might want to take your child's part to model a new behavior. Then switch roles and have your child try it.

12

Family Meetings: Yes, They Really Can Work!

"I've been amazed at how easy it has been to start family meetings. I'd been avoiding it for some time because it sounded so complicated. I discovered it doesn't have to be, and it's a great excuse to touch base with each other in a different way than we do ordinarily."

—Colleen, parent of two

"Thanks for the refresher on family meetings. We tried one a few years ago and it was a disaster. The kids wouldn't sit still, and we barraged them with a list of problems and frustrations and let them know what had to change around here. It ended in tears, and none of us wanted a repeat. This time we called for a powwow to talk about how things are going and ended with dessert, a rare treat at our house. What a difference!"

—Mitch, parent of seven

"The best thing about family meetings for me has been the amazing difference it has made in how discipline and sibling issues are solved at our house. From the moment we posted the agenda and wrote down complaints to bring up at the meeting, the burden was lifted from me, the parent who's usually at home to hear about all the fights. I no longer feel responsible for solving every problem on the spot. Instead we've been

working on problem solving when we're all together and cooled off. What a relief. Thanks!"
                                          —Martha, parent of three

THESE ARE TYPICAL SAMPLES OF FEEDBACK FROM PARENTS IN RESPONSE to our classwork on family meetings. It's not unusual for parents to feel somewhat reluctant about attempting family meetings. Often they're afraid it will be too complicated or time-consuming and will fill their already busy schedule with one more obligation. Some tried family meetings once or twice with mixed results and simply didn't make it a priority to continue. A few adults have negative memories from their own childhoods, when their parents held a family gathering in order to scold and to demand better behavior.

When we first taught parenting classes, we showed a commercial video of a family meeting. The carefully written script was awkwardly performed by semiprofessional actors. The children behaved perfectly, everyone always listened carefully and said the right thing, and they all agreed in the end. Each time we showed it, we felt a little uncomfortable. This certainly wasn't what family meetings in *our* homes were like, and we worried about the expectations we were creating in our class members.

So we decided to take the plunge and videotape one of our own family meetings. We knew that, if nothing else, we could count on our kids to be real. Viewing a live family in action might give people some practical ideas about how to do it themselves. It could also help do away with delusions about ideal families, delusions that are responsible for so much guilt and frustration. This is how Jeanne remembers it:

Our idea of sharing one of our family meetings with our parenting class was a great concept, no doubt, but all our ideals didn't prepare me for the moment of truth. When I popped the video into the machine that night, it was with mixed feelings. The home video I had made the previous weekend was a far cry from the perfectly scripted family meetings we'd shown in previous classes.

The scene opened with all of us gathered around the table in our small-but-cozy dining room. My son, Andy, who was nine years old then, was facilitating, using a simple outline of the meeting structure to help him remember what to do. It was my husband John's week to be the recorder, and he was poised, pen in hand, ready to write down our brainstorms and to record in our family-council notebook any decisions we made. As the first minute whizzed by, we tried to get the meeting started amid the chaos of kids making faces and joking for the camera. Andy asked if there were any further items for the agenda, which we keep posted on the refrigerator so that people can add items as they come up.

Anna Marie, who was almost five, settled into drawing with crayons and paper. We'd been having family meetings since she was three, and we had found that she would sit through the meeting happily if her hands were busy. Occasionally she would make a contribution and then return to her work.

"Any old business?" Andy asked. The overly ambitious agenda included checking in to see how chores were going, negotiating Andy's allowance, naming the new car, figuring out a way to thank the man who had helped us fix our flat tire on the highway, and planning a family activity.

In our discussion of the chores, the core issue was Andy's memory lapses about getting his jobs done. After a brief discussion we brainstormed a list of ideas: Give Andy one large job to do rather than several small ones; try harder to remember; put a picture or note under his dinner plate to remind him to do his chores after dinner; ground him for forgetting to do his jobs; have Andy hire someone to do his jobs for him; or have Andy hire someone to remind him to do the jobs.

Andy led us through an evaluation of each item. Midway he stopped and said, "Anna Marie, get your thumb out of your mouth." Responding with a defiant grin, she stuck her thumb farther in. "Okay," he came back, self-schooled in reverse psychology, "leave your finger in your mouth." Again the defiant grin, and she took it out. Andy rolled his eyes, and the meeting went on.

After some struggle we all agreed that a job-reminder place mat would be the best idea. "Who's going to make it?" I inquired. Silence. Then Andy pointed at me. "I'll do it, but will you help me?" I said.

"All right."

"I want to help," chimed in Anna Marie. Andy proceeded to act out his best rendition of someone who was dying an instant death by choking. I suggested that she might make some flowers around the edges. The meeting continued. Anna Marie gyrated around in her chair now and again, and then settled back into her drawing. The sibling banter continued, but still we somehow managed to move successfully through our business.

I turned off the VCR, curious about how the class would respond.

"Do your kids always act like that?" came the first question from the class.

"They were a little keyed up for the video, but basically that's how our meetings go," I responded.

"We could do that!" another parent joined in. "Somehow I thought it had to be different. More formal or something."

This attitude is typical of parents who've been unsure about their ability to run a family meeting. But once they overcome their initial resistance, give it a try, and notice the results, they're usually committed. It's not long before they wonder how they ever handled things before family meetings and why they were reluctant to try them in the first place.

THE BENEFITS OF FAMILY MEETINGS

Some of the effects of meetings are realized immediately, whereas other benefits emerge over the long haul. Once a routine is established, the family meeting becomes even more central to how the family functions, and the payoffs multiply. We've noticed the advantages listed below emerging in our own families and in the families we know who have instituted regular family meetings. Some of the benefits of family meetings are that they:

• **Establish an ongoing forum for resolving conflicts creatively.** When conflicts arise during the week, all family members can anticipate the family meeting as a time where everyone will be heard and problems will be tackled constructively. Conflicts are less likely to be managed by old reactive patterns when a clear plan is in place to manage them. We're also more likely to be creative in resolving conflicts when we practice these skills together.

• **Create a neutral time and place to deal with emotional issues after feelings have cooled.** Family meetings naturally allow for cooling off between the time of the conflict and the time for its resolution. As a result emotions are less likely to interfere with the problem-solving process. Conflicts sometimes lose their importance as time passes, and the parties involved may no longer even feel the need to address them by the time the meeting occurs.

• **Give kids a structure for practicing decision making.** This is one of the most important skills children can carry to adulthood.

Regular practice in a safe environment on real, everyday issues gives children fertile opportunities to develop these skills.

- **Provide a time for family organization.** Planning of chores, logistics of transportation, and working out family calendars can be handled effectively in family meetings. Having a regular time for planning reduces family stress and improves communication among busy family members.

- **Establish shared responsibility for family decisions.** When you share the power in making some decisions, you as a parent do not always have to play the heavy.

- **Promote family unity and teamwork.** When children see their family working together on a regular basis to resolve conflicts, they learn valuable lessons about cooperation and compromise. This teamwork strengthens family bonds.

- **Enlist cooperation by involving everyone in making decisions.** Children are much more likely to comply with the decisions they've helped make. There is little need to rebel against a policy they've helped form, and power struggles are minimized.

- **Provide opportunities to practice communication skills.** The motivation for mastering listening, speaking, and writing skills is high when children see the effect they can have on the decisions that affect their lives.

GETTING ORGANIZED FOR FAMILY MEETINGS

Family meetings come in all shapes and sizes. Some are low-key, with the family informally doing business and problem solving over dinner. Others are much more formal and structured. The format will grow and change with your family.

When Susan's family started holding family meetings, they needed a formal structure to establish the problem-solving process. They met every Monday night, no matter what. Now that the kids are older, they problem-solve more informally over dinner and they hold meetings every two weeks to share calendars and settle allowances. When bigger issues come up, they still use a formal council to tackle the problem.

There's no "right" way to do it. Decide on a style and format that works for your family.

WHEN?

Particularly at first it's helpful to pick a regular meeting time, perhaps weekly or bimonthly. Busy families who have difficulty finding a regular time to meet sometimes use focused dinnertime discussion as an alternative. One family struggling with the scheduling issue chose to meet over lunch at a local sandwich shop. As an added bonus, the kids were so impressed by having Saturday lunch out that they worked harder during the meeting to take care of business. Another family of a very active and distractible six-year-old found that their meetings needed to be more formal and focused. This gave important training about staying on track in order to finish the business at hand. They always celebrated afterward, often going out for frozen yogurt.

Most families find that convening regularly is essential to successful family forums. The key is to establish a *consistent* structure, be it formal or informal, for resolving conflicts, for planning, and for making decisions. We received this feedback from a class participant:

> When we first started a family council, we'd meet on Saturday mornings off and on. We weren't very consistent about meeting at a regular time. But after about a year we started to see how even irregular sessions were paying off. We've been meeting more regularly for the past two years. Although we still sometimes skip a week or two now and again, we all see family meetings as one of our family routines, and we know we can count on that time to get organized, work on problems, and have fun together.

HOW?

In deciding on a style and format that works for your family, consider some of the following basic ingredients:

- **Designating a facilitator and a recorder.** The facilitator keeps the meeting on track, and the recorder takes notes to establish an ongoing record of family decisions. Responsibility for running the meeting can be rotated among family members once everyone understands how the meetings work. Keeping a basic list of the usual order of business will help fledgling leaders learn to run meetings themselves.

- **Making an agenda.** A list can be posted on the refrigerator or other public place for writing down issues as they arise between meetings. As the meeting begins, ask, "Does anyone have any items to put on the agenda?"

- **Checking in on past decisions.** Take time to review solutions from previous meetings. Is there a need for further discussion or refinement?

- **Discussing new items.** Sometimes a discussion that airs and clarifies an issue is enough to resolve a concern. When it's appropriate, use the problem-solving process to address conflicts. *Be sure to decide ahead of time whether the issue is one that you as a parent are willing to open up for family discussion.* If your child puts an issue on the agenda that you feel needs to be a parental decision, say so ("We can talk about this at our meeting today, but I'm not comfortable turning this decision over to the whole family.").

- **Listening to all family members.** Everyone in the family should be given the opportunity to express his or her feelings and ideas on each issue.

- **Deciding by consensus.** Decisions are usually made by consensus. If agreement can't be reached, the issue is tabled until the next meeting. Sometimes a tentative consensus can be reached by asking reluctant participants, "Would you be willing to try this for a week?" If the answer is no, your response might be, "If we can't make a decision on this as a family, then I'll have to decide for you."

- **Expressing appreciation and celebrating accomplishments.** Many families express appreciation and celebrate accomplishments as a part of their regular order of business. This creates an encouraging atmosphere and helps build family unity.

WHAT?

Family meetings can be used to resolve conflicts; to plan family activities; to organize routines; to communicate organizational information (calendar, transportation, etc.); to celebrate, share, and play. Here's an agenda from one of Susan's family meetings:

AGENDA

Celebrations and appreciations

Scheduling

Old business:

1. Messes left in living room

New business:

1. Naming the puppy
2. Deciding who will feed the cats next door
3. Plan fun family activity

Pay allowances

Many families end meetings with refreshments, a game, or another enjoyable activity. Having something to look forward to often helps the business move along more vigorously.

GETTING STARTED: THE FIRST MEETING

Diana couldn't wait to check in with the rest of the group the week after our session on family meetings:

> "I didn't really expect our first attempt at a family meeting to go so well. I'm in a new marriage, and my new husband hasn't been around kids that much, so I was really glad that we saw your video before trying it on our own. The first thing we did in our meeting was to plan an outing. Then I suggested that each of us share one thing we liked about each person. It worked! I couldn't believe it! Even my nine-year-old son, who never says anything nice, gave his seven-year-old sister a sincere compliment. I sat there with tears streaming down my face, I was so happy and so relieved. We

played a game after that and had a great time. What a
great way to get our family started on the right foot!"

Diana recognized the importance of creating a positive attitude
toward the family-meeting routine from the start. Since it's wise to
keep the first meeting simple and enjoyable, planning a family activity is a good beginning agenda. Parents should facilitate the first
meetings, until children become familiar with the meeting routine.
Later even children as young as four can facilitate a meeting with
prompting from a parent.
Establish simple ground rules, such as:

1. No put-downs.
2. Everyone has the right to speak without being interrupted.
3. Avoid blaming.

In some families the rules are read at the beginning of each meeting. When a rule is broken, simply restate it to get the offender
back on track: "Remember, no put-downs at family meetings."
Soon your children will make sure that everyone remembers the
ground rules.
After the first meeting create an agenda that meets the needs of
your family. In a few weeks everyone will know what to expect,
and the meetings should flow more smoothly. Slowly work up to
bigger issues and longer meetings. Check the tips at the end of
this chapter periodically to refresh yourself and to avoid annoying
setbacks.
From the beginning set up a notebook to keep a written record
of your meetings. When there is disagreement later about the outcome of a decision, the family-meeting book is an invaluable reference. It also becomes a cherished piece of family history as the
years go by.

Family Meetings for All Ages

Part of designing a meeting to suit your family includes consid-
eration of the ages of your children. If your children are very
young, keep the meetings short and playful. Your "meeting" might
simply be participating in an enjoyable family activity. When you
feel your children are ready, use the meeting to plan a family activity for a later time. If you're dealing with preschoolers, flexibility
is important. Most of them will have difficulty sitting still and lis-

tening for more than a few minutes, especially if the discussion does not concern them. Around age four, children are usually developmentally ready to participate in the problem-solving process. Until then these simple beginnings will lay the foundation for more serious business as your children grow older. They will learn to anticipate family meetings happily, and this positive attitude will be invaluable later.

If your children cover a wide range of ages, try giving the younger ones something to do with their hands (crayons, puzzles, or small building toys) to keep them sitting with you. They may lose interest and wander away. Let them go. You might want to put the business that would most concern younger children at the beginning of the agenda.

Teenagers may provide a different challenge. Their need for independence from the family sometimes makes them reluctant contributors. Let them know that they can choose not to attend, but that decisions that are made *will be binding for the family*, including issues directly involving them. If you haven't shared decision making in the past, it may take some time before they trust your sincerity. Once you've developed the routine and proven that you will stick to it, you'll gain their trust. Family meetings are also a great place to negotiate the use of the car, if everyone comes equipped with their weekly calendar.

TIPS FOR HOLDING FAMILY MEETINGS

A few tips may help to ensure your success with family meetings. From time to time, review these basic guidelines to avoid pitfalls:

- **Review ground rules as the need arises during the meeting or before you begin.**

- **Strive to keep the meetings short, setting priorities beforehand.**

- **Be clear about what issues you're comfortable turning over to the group.** Some issues, such as those concerning health and safety, are not negotiable.

- **Try to stay away from the role of "parent as boss" during the family meeting.** Avoid announcing unilateral decisions at the meeting. If you have difficulty with this, spend time beforehand deciding what is negotiable and what is not. Let your kids

5156
45

facilitate the meetings once they understand the format. Also, when you're problem solving, let the kids take the lead in brainstorming ideas.

• **A light tone will create a positive atmosphere, and family members will begin to look forward to future meetings.**

• **If you have difficulty engaging your spouse's support for family meetings, just begin the process alone.** Positive results are sometimes enough to bring a reluctant spouse on board.

• **Avoid making the meeting a dumping ground for complaints by choosing carefully when and how to approach bigger issues, focusing on solutions rather than on blame.**

• **If agreement is difficult to reach, ask if everyone would be willing to try a new way for a week.**

• **Keep a sense of humor!**

Practicing

1. Get started. Plan a first family meeting, following the guidelines in this chapter. Remember to limit the agenda to an easily attainable and appealing goal, such as choosing a family activity.

2. Write about or think about the process of making decisions in your family. Are the adults responsible for most of the decisions? What areas of decision making can be shared with your children?

3. How much responsibility did you have as a child for decisions? How would you have felt if you had been invited to participate in the process? Write about it in your journal.

4. If you've struggled with family meetings in the past, explore the reasons why. Using the information in this chapter, make a plan to overcome the problems you experienced. Share your plan with a friend or parenting partner and check back after you've tried it.

5. Discuss at a family meeting ways your family can reward itself for holding meetings regularly (for example, going to a movie to celebrate success).

6. After you've established regular meetings, try new locations. What effect does the setting have on the quality of the meeting? Where are meetings most likely to be successful for your family?

13
Parenting Partnerships: Sticking Together Even When You Disagree

Nancy and Ed were married for eight years before starting a family. When they first met, they were delighted by their differences and saw their love as proof of the attraction-of-opposites theory. Their prechild marriage was relatively harmonious, but their conflicts increased with each year of parenthood. By the time their youngest entered grade school, they rarely had a conversation about the kids that didn't end with accusations and hurt feelings. They knew that their children needed them to get a handle on the situation.

NANCY AND ED'S PREDICAMENTS HAVE A FAMILIAR RING TO MANY STRUG-gling couples. Their conflicts had roots in countless differences: family history, personal temperament, and communication styles, to name a few. Ed, an only child of older, traditional parents, was used to having a great deal of control over his environment. His conflict style was **directing,** and his job in management required him to be a quick problem solver. He often felt responsible for making the kids toe the line, and he was frustrated with Nancy's "soft" style.

Nancy, on the other hand, grew up in a lively and somewhat disorganized household with eight children. When confronted with conflict she was likely to **accommodate** or to **avoid** the problem. As a social worker she had developed skills at listening and empathizing. These were a blessing and a curse in her interactions with her children, who could talk to her about their problems, but who sometimes manipulated her into allowing them to do what they wanted to do. Because Nancy's father had been authoritarian, she rebelled against Ed's edicts and didn't feel comfortable enforcing them when she was the parent in charge.

Nancy saw Ed as a rigid and unreasonable disciplinarian. Ed saw Nancy as being spineless. She called him controlling. He accused her of encouraging the kids' irresponsibility by being tolerant of their chaos. She said he never listened to anybody else's point of view, especially hers or the kids'. He countered by suggesting she'd blow whichever way the wind blew, regardless of what was best for the family. He wondered why he always had to play the bad guy. She said he didn't have to play that part, he chose it. And so it went.

Many couples fall into patterns of conflict over child-rearing issues. Often spouses will polarize, as Nancy and Ed did. Nancy became more lenient in response to Ed's rigidity, and Ed responded by tightening the reins even more. Nancy would slip into the kids' room after Ed laid down one of his pronouncements and she'd lessen the severity of the punishment to make it easier on them. As a result she came to establish a closeness with the kids that pushed Ed farther away from them. This is a typical pattern: One parent forms an alliance with the child or children, which further polarizes the adults, and the left-out parent withdraws even more from the family.

Most of these kinds of struggles can be effectively addressed through the teamwork of parents. A good working relationship provides both partners with a sounding board and the support and perspective they need. This alliance also gives kids clear and reassuring messages about parents working together, willing and able to provide the thoughtful leadership children need.

ROADBLOCKS TO TEAMWORK

Through counseling, Ed and Nancy were able to understand their differing styles and the influence of their family backgrounds. They recognized that they were stuck in a power struggle over who was going to "win." It was important to both of them to be "right," and their disagreements turned into ego battles over who had the best judgment. Ed's fears of the kids' being ruined by Nancy's "indulgent" parenting fanned the flames of the conflict.

Other parents get into trouble by believing that they must always think, act, and be alike when it comes to dealing with their children. As a result they spend a great deal of time trying to convince the other person to do it their way. While teamwork is important, differences in child-rearing styles are inevitable, and they can actually be a positive influence on the family if parents are working together.

EFFECTIVE PARENTING TEAMWORK

The strategies Ed and Nancy developed to deal with their problem are useful for any parents who wish to strengthen their teamwork:

- **Listening skills.** Temporarily suspending your personal agenda and truly hearing your partner's fears and concerns are cornerstones of strong parent teamwork. Attentive listening, discussed in Chapter 10, creates an atmosphere of mutual support. Keep in mind, though, that there are as many differences in styles of communication as there are in styles of conflict. New research indicates that gender differences may have a significant effect on couple communication. Expecting your partner to listen the way you prefer may defeat your teamwork.

- **Problem solving.** Mutual problem solving puts both parents on the same team. Using the process described in Chapter 10, parents can find solutions that address the concerns of both parties. Often these brainstormed solutions are unique and creative, the result of two people pooling their experience and mental resources. If playful suggestions are encouraged, brainstorming can add humor to the situation and to the couple relationship. When parents problem-solve effectively, no one is blamed, and both partners let go of the need to be right or to be the expert. "Action Plan for Change," Appendix B, is intended to help parents through the process of taking more leadership with their children. You might also want to use "Peacing It Together: The Tools," Appendix C, to help you generate ideas and to remind you of all the ideas we've offered in the book.

- **Nurturing your relationship as a couple.** Being a parent is hard work. Doing the job well can be so demanding that it's easy to neglect your relationship as a couple. Your couple connection is the foundation upon which your family is built. Talk together, play together, and plan special times to enjoy each other's company without the children.

• **Sticking together.** When your partner is in the midst of a conflict with a child, it's tempting to give advice about how to manage the situation. Resist. Open disagreement may confuse your kids and demoralize your partner. Differences of opinion can be discussed at another time, away from the stressful situation and the children.

• **Respecting differences.** Most couples can find a few basic family rules to agree on, such as not allowing physical violence or expecting the kids to call home if they will be arriving later than planned. Although this list will be different for different families, it is important to have solidarity on a few basic issues of mutual concern.

Because differences in personal child-rearing styles are inevitable, in many cases parents can agree to disagree without disastrous consequences. It *is* important to talk about these differences to sort out which ones you can let go and which ones you need to negotiate. Ed and Nancy started to tangle one night about how to pack for their vacation. Nancy always packed the children's bags for trips. It was faster for her to do it herself than to supervise the kids' haphazard efforts. Ed accused her of doing too much for the kids and said that they should pack their own bags. They were at it again.

Remembering one of the suggestions their counselor had made, Nancy said, "Okay, we disagree on this one. Let's take some time to cool off and talk about it after lunch."

Later they took a short walk and discussed the disagreement. "I'm feeling really stressed out by all this packing and getting ready, and I want to make sure the kids bring the right things along," Nancy began.

"You're always babying them. They need to learn to do some things for themselves," Ed retorted.

Nancy felt hurt, and she felt her internal radiator heating up. She used self-talk to avoid reacting and to stay focused on the problem. After a minute she said, "I know you think that. I've heard you say it before, but I'm really just trying to make it easier on me."

This time Ed seemed to hear her concern. "How about if I take charge of supervising the kids while they pack? That will free you to do the other stuff you need to do."

"But what if they forget to pack something they really need?" she said worriedly.

"Why don't you give me a list of things you really don't want them to forget?" Ed suggested.

Nancy reflected for a minute, once again using self-talk: *Is this something I can let go of? What would be the worst thing that could happen? I guess if they forget something we can always pick it up at a store on the way.*

"Sounds like it might work. I guess I'd be willing to try it this time," she answered.

When there is open communication between partners, these differences can become an asset instead of a problem. Ed's perspective helped Nancy allow the children to be more independent in situations like this. A teamwork attitude between parents strengthens the family by encouraging different perspectives, and it gives everyone opportunities to practice flexibility. Parenting partnership meetings, informal or formal, are great places to work out these differences of opinion.

GETTING STARTED WITH PARENTING-PARTNERSHIP MEETINGS

Ed and Nancy decided to set aside once a week on Sunday nights after the kids were in bed to talk about parenting issues. They also used this time to make decisions about other family business, such as finances and vacation planning.

As their communication improved, Ed and Nancy felt ready to tackle a family-problem area. At first they had so many areas of frustration, they didn't know which to choose. They asked themselves which single change would reduce tension and save their energy the most.

Bedtime hassles won hands down. After some discussion they decided that this was an issue they needed to stand firm on together and that it wasn't open to negotiation with the children. They set guidelines for bedtime and agreed on which consequences they'd use if the kids didn't cooperate. Since the next day was Saturday, they decided to let the kids in on their plan at breakfast.

The next morning Nancy announced, "We've been making some mistakes, and we're going to start doing some things differently."

Ed took the ball: "Bedtimes are a hassle for us. When nine o'clock rolls around, we're tired, and we need to have some time alone together. We get really frustrated when you stall around getting ready for bed and then get up several times before you finally go to sleep. From now on everyone needs to be in bed with lights out at nine o'clock. We only want to hear from you if there's an emergency. Once you're tucked in, each time you call us to your room or get out of bed, you will go to bed ten minutes earlier the next evening. That way you can pay us back for the time together that your mother and I lost."

Ed invited the children to share their insights and ideas for a smoother bedtime transition. After some brainstorming they made a plan for a bedtime routine that incorporated the children's ideas, such as having a special family storytime at eight-thirty and celebrating after a week of success by going to the skating rink. They wrote down the whole bedtime plan and posted it on the refrigerator.

The next night at dinner Ed reminded the kids of the agreement, "Tonight is the first night we try our new plan. Everyone remember what we talked about?"

At bedtime that night the routine went more smoothly than ever before. Nancy and Ed heaved a mutual sigh of relief and enjoyed a quiet evening together.

As the days passed, however, things didn't always go so smoothly. That's when Ed and Nancy really began to appreciate the support they had learned to give each other. When Nancy started to weaken in following through with the consequences, Ed gently reminded her of the importance of what they were doing and the positive effect it was having on their family and on their relationship. One night, when Ed got really angry at the kids for delaying bedtime another fifteen minutes, he realized that he needed to cool off. Nancy supported him by taking over while he went for a walk. Although the change wasn't miraculous, the long-term bedtime situation definitely improved. Once the change was well established, the family went on to resolve other issues.

USING THE PARENTING-PARTNERSHIP MEETING TO HEAD
OFF PROBLEMS

Ed and Nancy discovered the value of their meetings for *anticipating* problems. Many long-standing conflicts were headed off with a little advance planning. In early June they addressed the changes in routine that would occur when school was out for the summer. They clarified which rules they were willing to leave open to negotiation and which ones weren't negotiable. Next they held a family meeting for input on issues that were negotiable. As a result of this teamwork the transition to summer was the smoothest in years.

While Ed and Nancy chose to set up a structured time to talk, other couples use different approaches. A casual conversation over dinner or during a walk may suffice. Be aware that if you choose the more informal approach, the temptation to avoid conflict is usually strong enough that you may find that you never get around to resolving or discussing differences of opinion. In addition, without a regular routine for dealing with business, details of parenting may eat up much of the time that you're together, reducing the time spent simply enjoying each other's company. There are benefits to having a framework, even if it's not a formal one. Some couples find that keeping an agenda and taking notes on agreements, as in a family meeting, helps keep the meetings focused and efficient.

Establishing a few ground rules may be useful. Here's a list that one couple shared with us:

• Focus on problems, not on each other's character traits.

• All feelings are accepted.

• Avoid blaming.

• If an issue seems hot, table it for a week. Avoid talking about it while you're angry.

One couple who had particular difficulty discussing "hot" issues agreed that these issues would be discussed but no decisions made until the following week. The time in between allowed them to think about the problem with a new perspective and to observe themselves and their kids in the situations under dispute.

For families with two parents in the home, the couple bond is the most important link in developing a healthy climate. Maintaining a strong partnership goes a long way toward making home a safe and peaceable place to grow.

STICKING TOGETHER EVEN IF YOU DON'T STAY TOGETHER

If you're living in different households, it's even more important to work on clear communication on child-rearing issues. Find your common ground of concerns and try to come to agreement over basic expectations and rules. Many of the stories and tips in this chapter are still relevant to your situation.

If your relationship with your spouse is heavily laden with emotion, use self-talk to avoid heating up and to stay focused on the problem. Decide which issues are the most important and let go of trying to control the small stuff. Concerns over your children's safety, such as letting them ride with a dangerous driver or keeping them out so late that they come back exhausted or ill, take precedence over what TV shows they're allowed to watch or whether they eat too much junk food.

If your children complain that "we don't have to do that at Mom's house," calmly respond, "These are the rules in this household. Your mom may have different rules at her place, but these are the rules here." Kids are adaptable. They'll adjust to the rules and learn about flexibility in the process.

If you're bringing up children by yourself without support from another adult, find someone with whom you can share your feelings and your trials as a parent. Use the problem-solving process to brainstorm answers to difficult issues.

TIPS FOR WORKABLE PARENTING PARTNERSHIPS

- **Set up a time to get together with your partner to clarify which issues are open to negotiation with the kids and which areas are nonnegotiable.**

- **Keep individual incidents in perspective.** It's easy to exaggerate the harm that your children suffered as a result of a situation you or your partner didn't handle well. Over the course of growing up, one minor incident won't have that much influence on their development.

- **Take responsibility for changing yourself, not your partner.** Admitting your part in creating the problem reduces the polarizing that easily occurs between two people.

- **Use feeling statements when discussing hot issues to keep communication clear and open with your parenting partner.**

- **Avoid the one-parent-as-expert syndrome.** It makes the other parent feel ineffective, and he may withdraw or abdicate the parenting role altogether.

- **Ask for help with your part of the problem.** When you admit you don't have all the answers, your partner is less likely to become defensive.

- **Share responsibility for enforcement as much as possible.** Neither parent likes to be considered the ogre in the family. As parents we can be each other's most valuable assets in creating peace at home. We can offer each other the kind of perspective and support available nowhere else.

Practicing

1. Ask your partner to take the conflict-styles inventory in Chapter 2, and share your results with each other.

2. Try out parenting-partnership meetings for a month. Explore different structures and styles to see what works best for you. At the end of a month talk about what did and didn't work. Decide how to continue from here.

3. Think of a "hot" issue you'd like to discuss with your partner. Imagine yourself bringing up the subject, using your best feeling statements and listening skills. Then try it.

4. Sit down with your partner and plan a special date sometime in the next week. Leave the kids at home and have a good time!

5. Take turns planning a surprise date for your partner. Advise him or her about what to wear for the activity and take care of the rest yourself. If you enjoy this, consider making it a monthly routine.

6. Try this listening-skills exercise with your partner: One at a time each person talks about himself or herself for fifteen minutes. Avoid talking about the other person or the relationship. Do not interrupt. When that partner is finished, the other one thanks him or her, but offers no advice. Then the other person talks. Discuss your experiences as listeners and as talkers.

7. Discuss the positive qualities of each individual child. Share your list with the child. Decide as a couple what one change you'd like to encourage in each child. Discuss ways you might support a change together.

8. As a couple choose an area of conflict with your kids that creates family stress. Use the chart "Action Plan for Change," Appendix B, to guide you in making a change together.

14

Preventing Conflict Before It Starts

"Our parenting class so far has been focused on problem solving and responding to difficult behaviors, which has been helpful. But tonight's class focusing on preventing conflict by using encouragement such as special time seems so much lighter and provides just the perspective I needed."

—*Mary, parent of three*

IF WE CREATE AN ENVIRONMENT THAT GIVES FAMILY MEMBERS A SENSE of belonging and significance, we can head off many conflicts. We foster a climate of respect, acceptance, and love by taking time to be together to listen and to share; by recognizing the uniqueness of family members: their strengths, their needs and their contributions; by working and playing together; and by seeing mistakes as opportunities to grow.

SPECIAL TIME

Gloria, a busy parent who worked part-time outside the home, sought the advice of her daughter Robin's preschool teacher when she noticed that for the past two weeks four-year-old Robin had been getting more and more physically aggressive, kicking and punching her three-year-old sister and her playmates at home and at preschool. Robin's teacher asked if there had been any changes at home recently. The warning bells went off in Gloria's head when she realized that for the past few weeks she'd been putting in many extra hours at work on an important project with a tight deadline.

Gloria decided to schedule a little special time with Robin for the duration of the project. That night she and Robin talked about going out for a doughnut the next day. Robin was suspicious at first that the date was going to be used to deliver another lecture on her negative behavior. Reassured that it was just for fun, she agreed to go. After a few days Gloria noticed a dramatic improvement in Robin's behavior. Also, they had such a good time together on these outings that the tradition continued even after Gloria's project was finished. In the future, when she had a choice, Gloria was careful about scheduling extra hours at work.

Special time is probably the single most effective strategy for reducing conflict. A regularly scheduled event where parent and child spend time together doing some pleasurable activity, special time can occur for twenty minutes or more once a week, or for five to ten minutes each day. A regularly scheduled special time not only gives your child something to look forward to but also assures her that spending time with her is a priority for you.

Let your child choose the activity. Ideas are limited only by time and by your imaginations. Read a favorite story, enjoy hot chocolate or a frozen-yogurt treat together, play a board game, roller-skate, create an art project, bake a cake, or play a round of tennis.

> *"At our house we incorporate special time into the bedtime routine. The day always ends with each child tucked in bed, sharing read-aloud time with a parent. After that each kid shares the best and worst thing that happened to him or her that day. We learn a lot about what our children are thinking and feeling from this."*
> *—Michael, father of three*

Special time is a unique opportunity to learn what's going on inside your child's head. Give her your total attention. Avoid lecturing or giving advice and focus on listening and enjoying each other. This is not a time to hammer home your pet peeve about your child's behavior. Because special time increases a child's sense of personal significance by strengthening his bond with individual parents, this strategy is especially helpful during times of stress or when you're working on making a change in your child's behavior.

LISTENING AND SHARING

Good listening helps our children feel understood and valued. When we truly listen, we put ourselves in our child's shoes and attempt to experience his point of view. Since most conflicts are caused by poor communication, attentive listening can help prevent potential rifts and short-circuit conflicts before they develop into full-blown problems. Refer to the basics covered in Chapter 10, and follow these general guidelines:

• Give nonverbal signals that show you are all ears (squat so that you can listen to your child at his level, make eye contact, postpone other tasks).

• Encourage your child to elaborate on her thinking ("Tell me more about that." "How did you feel when that happened?").

• Show you are listening and understanding what is being said by rephrasing or clarifying.

• Reflect the child's basic feelings about what he's sharing ("So you felt embarrassed when you gave the wrong answer in front of your class?").

• Paraphrase any agreements you reach to make sure you both share the same understanding.

Although it *is* useful to keep these general guidelines in mind, you don't have to consciously hit every tip on the list or carefully control the interaction in order to deescalate a conflict using these communication tools.

> One day Marie's fourteen-year-old son, Blake, was putting on his bike helmet to ride to tennis lessons when Marie noticed once again that a haircut was overdue. This was a "hot" topic between them. Even though Blake liked a new haircut once he had one, he preferred to spend his leisure time doing other things besides going to the barber. This sometimes resulted in

harassment or put-downs from his peers. Marie had discussed this before with Blake, and they'd agreed that he would try combing his hair with gel after he washed it to avoid getting it cut a little while longer. Just before he took off on his bike, Marie noticed that the new plan wasn't working and (perhaps unwisely!) chose this moment to address the issue.

"When are you going to get your hair cut?" she yelled from the front door.

"Mom, it really makes me mad when you bug me about my hair," Blake shot back.

Marie walked over to the driveway and made eye contact with Blake while he straddled his bike. She spoke matter-of-factly.

"I don't like it when I have to nag you, either, and I thought I could wait until you decided to do it on your own, but I can't seem to let go of it," she said. "Is your hair bugging you?"

"I guess so, mostly because you keep bringing it up. I guess it's just too much trouble to keep combing it," he answered.

"Since we're both getting sick of the nagging business, and I can't seem to let go of how your hair looks, how about a compromise: You agree to get it cut by the weekend, and I won't mention it anymore," Marie suggested.

"I guess so," Blake agreed.

"Okay. So you'll take care of it before we leave on the camping trip Friday at four. That'll give you three days. And I'll keep my mouth shut. Deal?"

"Okay. Gotta go to tennis. 'Bye," Blake answered.

The conversation took about a minute. Blake showed off his new haircut at dinner the following night.

Family psychologist John Taylor suggests a strategy for older children that incorporates attentive listening: Set aside time for a one-on-one interview. Ask what you can do differently to make his life go better. This gives the adolescent a safe time and place for airing gripes as well as a feeling that his perceptions are considered important. Listen carefully, without arguing back, to everything your teen suggests before offering one (and *only* one) request for a change from the child.

Taking time to share stories and personal experiences also strengthens family bonds. Children love to hear stories about your childhood. Discuss the things you value and why they're important to you. The thread of good communication can be woven through your daily interactions with your children. It is essential in creating an atmosphere where family members feel connected and valued.

ENHANCING COOPERATION

Developing a spirit of family cooperation fosters a climate where all are committed to the well-being of others in the family. Children learn their first lessons about social interest from this: We work together because we care about others, and in the end what is good for the community is good for all of us.

> Eight-year-old Noah and his four-year-old sister, Laurel, spent much of their time bickering about everything under the sun. Noah seemed to need to exert his superior size and power over his little sister, and strong-willed Laurel wasn't about to take it. A thoughtful aunt gave them a cooperative game for a holiday gift. They spent many conflict-free hours overcoming the dangers in the forest of their cooperative game. The difference in their interactions over the game was so noticeable that when Grandma came to visit, she commented on the change.

Several books currently on the market explain how to play cooperative games that require no special equipment (see Bibliography). Cooperative board games can be purchased commercially, or you can change games you already own by inventing new rules. For example play double solitaire with the goal of both players, working together, being to run out of cards. In other games the group can work together to beat the timer or to break their last best record. In Ping-Pong both players might challenge themselves to see how long they can keep a volley going. One family invented partner croquet at a family reunion, each adult-child pair playing with one ball.

You can also encourage cooperation with family projects such as planting a garden, making a giant submarine sandwich to share, having a group treasure hunt, or holding family cleanup sessions with a special dessert treat to celebrate when the job is done. When getting ready to launch a new project or when you're facing a transition or a major change, ask your family, "How can we help each other through this?" Before going on a recent vacation, Susan and George enlisted Ben and Johanna's cooperation by discussing one potential trouble spot beforehand: "On this trip we'll be doing two long days of driving. How can we help each other have a good time?" Everyone had the opportunity to speak, expressing their own needs and their ideas for helping others in the family to have fun. They decided to bring a small tape recorder with headphones for the kids to trade off. Each brought a book to read, and their car cooler was packed with everyone's favorite cold drinks. A book of car games and songs provided several rounds of group fun, and regular stretch stops helped shake out restless muscles. Needless to say, the trip was far smoother than their last one.

Take time to talk to your family about cooperation and promote it as a family value. Cooperation is one of the building blocks in a strong family identity.

BUILDING FAMILY IDENTITY

> *"A family is for helping each other out when you're having trouble."*
> —*Johanna, age nine*

The recent history of Susan's daughter, Johanna, is reflected in her definition of family. During the previous few months she'd been having difficulty with playground friendships. At dinner Susan, George, and Johanna's brother, Ben, would listen to her tales of woe and offer suggestions. Johanna had learned that one part of her family's identity was helping each other solve problems.

A strong, positive family identity gives children a cherished place to belong. Children who know they belong have less need to adopt the values and actions of others to prove themselves. As a result they may be more resistant to peer pressure in the adolescent years, reducing the risk of substance abuse, promiscuity, and teen suicide.

Trips to the drive-in movies in pajamas; barbecued hamburgers and watermelon on the Fourth of July; turkey, pumpkin pie, and mincemeat on Thanksgiving; snow ice cream at the first snowfall in winter; and homemade ice cream in the summer—most of us can call up memories from our own childhoods that reflect the unique qualities of our families of origin.

Family identity develops from traditions, treasured memories, and shared experiences. One of the joys of parenthood is passing on these traditions and creating our own unique family rituals, reflecting our own values and goals. These are a few of the traditions parents in our classes have shared:

• Schedule an evening at home for the family each week. Play games and have fun together.

• Volunteer as a family once a month in a local soup kitchen.

• On birthdays make a treasure hunt for the birthday person.

• Worship together.

• Read a good book aloud to each other on long car trips.

• Light a candle at dinner each night in honor of a person or event or to express appreciation to the cook.

• Invite other families to join you for an annual Memorial Day weekend softball game and picnic.

• Choose a date to celebrate the birthday of a favorite author or character each year.

• At the end of a family vacation or outing, have each person share a reminiscence about their favorite part of the trip.

As children grow and change, these traditions may also evolve, but through the ages and stages we weave the tapestry of our unique family identity by creating treasured memories.

DON'T FORGET THE POWER OF HUMOR

"I was having one of those days. It was eight o'clock in the evening, and I was looking forward to a long, hot bath once the kids were finally tucked in. Then everything fell apart all at the same time. The baby threw up all over me just at the moment Jake announced that he was supposed to bring snacks for his kindergarten class the next day. My middle-schooler, Angela, appeared in the kitchen all upset. She'd been working on a major homework project that was due the next day, and she couldn't possibly get it done without

a trip to the library. I was exhausted, and I could feel myself losing control.

Then for a split second I stepped outside of myself and surveyed the scene. It was as if I were in a sitcom on TV. I chuckled to myself when I thought about what a funny story this would make when I talked to my mom on the phone the next weekend. Somehow those few seconds of laughing at myself gave me the energy to come back into the chaos and wade through it. The hot bath came later than I'd originally planned, but it never felt better."
—Sheila, parent of three

This parent discovered the value of humor. When she stepped out of her crisis of the moment, her sense of humor restored her energy and gave her a fresh perspective. Humor is one of the greatest gifts we can bring to parenting. In addition to being a valuable C.H.O.I.C.E.S. strategy, it renews our energy and restores our joy in life.

KEEP EXPECTATIONS REALISTIC

"When Matthew was ten, his disposition was delightful. His sense of humor blossomed; he was cooperative and fun to be around. Then, just after his eleventh birthday, he began to change. His moods swung like a pendulum. He flew off the handle easily, and he bad-mouthed his mother and me. I was wondering where we'd gone wrong with this kid and was starting to really clamp down on him, which only seemed to make things worse.

Then a friend loaned us a book about the developmental changes that kids go through from age nine to fourteen. Wow, was that a revelation! I could see that Matthew was being a typical eleven-year-old. While we still didn't tolerate the smart-mouth stuff, I could relax a little and give him some space to move through this rocky stage. Sure enough, about seven months later he was still showing signs of budding adolescence, but he was becoming much easier to live with again."
—Dennis, parent of one

Sometimes information about what other kids our child's age are doing can help us understand our own child's behavior. It's helpful to know that some stages are generally regarded as more difficult than others. For instance one of the developmental tasks of many four-year-olds seems to be testing boundaries. They need to feel a strong sense of personal power, which often manifests itself in physical aggression and superhero play. It helps if parents understand this stage when their formerly sweet three-year-old blossoms into a robust and energetic four who frequently tests the limits.

Research from the Gesell Institute teaches us about the pattern of growth and consolidation that can be seen throughout the growing-up years. Two-and-a-half-year-olds are notoriously difficult to live with as they push for independence. Extremes of behavior are not unusual. One minute the child may cling to a parent and the next minute she'll refuse to come to her. The cycle shifts in the third year, when the child consolidates the growth of the first years and is relatively easy to handle. The fourth year is again tumultuous, and so the cycle goes. Not all children hit these stages at the same age, and some children hit them harder than others. Knowing your own child will help you recognize where she is in her developmental cycle.

Books on ages and stages of children's growth are included in the Bibliography. Use these materials as a guide to help you decide how much autonomy is appropriate for your child. All children are different, and yours may be able to handle more autonomy than others his age. On the other hand he may need more structure or support than other children. Some children will be ready for more responsibility in some areas and need more structure in others. Once again, trust your instinctive understanding of your child.

Keep in mind that the transition from one age or stage to another is often difficult. At the same time that children are making a movement forward, they are often less secure or self-confident. Their contradictory behavior may make them harder to live with until the new stage is mastered.

CARING FOR YOUR CHILDREN MEANS CARING FOR YOURSELF

"When my life approaches maximum r.p.m., I sometimes find myself venting frustration about problems that occur elsewhere in my life on the kids.

They of course do the same thing. Conflict-prevention approaches are great; but I'm continually under pressure to be proactive in so many ways, every day, all week. The message is, I guess, that I need continually to keep reaching down more deeply within myself when there is conflict on all sides, even when I am pretty sure I have nothing left to give. When I feel drained, I need to take time to fill myself up again so that I can be the kind of dad I want to be; after all, kids are mirrors of ourselves and the real world.

—Andrew, parent of two

All too often parents find their personal needs drop to last on the priority list with the pressing demands of jobs, running a household, and raising kids. Our ability to nurture is greatly increased, however, if we make time during the busy week to do the things we love to do.

Sometimes this is easier said than done. According to Urie Bronfenbrenner, professor of Human Ecology at Cornell University, "The main problem in our society is that people are expected to raise children in their spare time." Parenting does take time, and if we overload our lives with too many commitments, our energy and patience are stretched thin. This may be the most lethal trap we face as parents.

We can reach deep within only if we allow ourselves the time to do it. Although the temptation to eliminate refueling time is always there, we can give our kids no better model than a parent who is willing to tend to himself or herself.

All the new conflict-resolution strategies in the world won't work if you don't allow yourself the reflective time necessary to integrate them. That's why it's so important to make small changes. Allowing yourself to burn out is the worst thing you can do for your family climate. Follow the hints in "How to Use This Book" to pace yourself. Stay focused on one issue at a time. In the next chapter you'll see how several parents develop one-step-at-a-time plans for handling five classic family conflicts. But don't start reading it yet. Go take a warm bath or do whatever you love to do most.

Practicing

1. Make a list of ten things you love to do. Set aside at least thirty minutes this week and do something from your list.

2. Complete a cooperative family project. Use your own idea or try one suggested in this chapter.

3. Plan a special time with each of your children sometime in the next week. Let your child choose the activity and remember to give her your full attention.

4. If you're having difficulty understanding a particular child, check out a book from the library on the developmental expectations for children that age (check the bibliography for selected titles). How does this change the way you see your child? Share your discoveries with your partner or a friend.

5. At dinner or at a family meeting share funny stories about an embarrassing or silly thing that happened to you. Look for humorous new material in your life as a parent.

15
Classic Conflicts, Peaceable Solutions

"What helps me most is hearing how other parents are handling problems. This gives me ideas for how I could do things differently. I've done a lot of reading, and most of the techniques discussed are familiar to me, but I always seem to run out of ideas when the problems are close to home."

—*Kay, parent of four in a blended family*

LIKE KAY, MANY OF US HAVE GATHERED A MULTITUDE OF CHILD-REARING strategies, but when we are confronted with a specific situation in our own homes, all the good ideas fly out the window. That's why one of the things parents enjoy most is coming together to pool parental wisdom and to create new and original solutions.

In this chapter we'll take a close-up look at some typical daily conflicts to see how parents come up with peaceable solutions that meet their family's distinctive needs. We'll share brainstormed ideas and point out a few things you might consider in deciding what will work for your family. In addition we'll show you how real parents put some of the things they learned in this book to work.

PUTTING TOGETHER YOUR PLAN

As you decide how to address a problem area, use the "Action Plan for Change" in Appendix B. It will guide you step-by-step through the conflict-resolution process.

Parents in our classes also use a summary list of brainstorming strategies we call "Peacing It Together: The Tools," Appendix C. Usually, once the ideas start flowing, inventing a plan that will work for you becomes much easier.

Once you've brainstormed a list of ideas, you might evaluate them using the Three *R*s or the question, "What might happen if we do this?" Which ideas are age appropriate and are workable, given the temperament of your child? Which ideas will balance your typical conflict-resolution style? Which ideas are practical, given your schedule and lifestyle? What are you willing to do, based on your personal values and beliefs?

CHORES

Conflicts in this area usually cluster around deciding who will do what and how to get chores done with minimal reminding. In our own families we find that an occasional revamp of our chore plan reenergizes the kids for attacking their jobs. When chores are neglected, or when complaining is on the rise, it's time to revisit the plan.

In her book *Pick Up Your Socks* parent educator Elizabeth Crary suggests that as you develop a family chore plan, you consider why having kids do chores is important to you. Is it to teach children how to do household tasks? To share the workload? To give kids an opportunity to contribute to the family? To teach them responsibility? How you answer might affect how you organize and divvy up chores. For instance if your primary goal is to teach children how to do different household tasks, you might rotate jobs frequently so that children practice a variety of tasks. If your goal is to share the workload, your plan might include giving kids tasks for longer periods of time so that you don't have to spend as much time training and supervising.

Don't expect kids to embrace chores wholeheartedly. After all, how many adults would put housework first on their personal hit parade? But it *is* important for kids to do chores, and some fresh ideas can lessen the burden for all family members.

One night class participants asked for a general brainstorm session on getting kids to do chores. Here are their ideas:

• Draw chores out of a hat.

• Divide up tasks by making a pocket chart with pictures of chores (for younger kids).

- The family could start doing chores together.

- Do chores at the same time every week or every day.

- Play "race the clock" when doing chores.

- Make a chart and have kids check off jobs or put up their own stars.

- Set a timer.

- Break a larger chore, such as room cleaning, into smaller tasks to help the child complete it (pick up floor, make bed, clear desk, put toys away, hang up clothes).

- Hire someone to do all the chores.

- Be sure to train kids carefully so that they know how to do the tasks.

- Parents go on strike.

- Use "When you _____, then you _____"; for example, "When your chores are done, then you can (go out to play, turn the TV on, etc.)."

- Kid pays mom or dad to do his chores.

- Don't worry about getting chores done.

- Bring in an imaginary big blue bunny to help do the chores.

- Make a robot that does chores.

- Set a time deadline for getting chores done.

- Make a deal with your kids that if you nag them more than once, you have to do their job.

- If child doesn't get chores done on time, mom or dad does the chore, and child owes them time.

- Problem-solve with the family to come up with a plan.

- If chore isn't done in timely manner, child is interrupted in whatever he or she is doing to get it done.

- Child could do chores with a friend or trade chores with a family member.

• Plan a special family game or other activity to do when all the chores are done.

• Have each child be in charge of cleaning a room of the house for a week.

• Pretend you are preparing for the arrival of the queen.

Two parents in the group used this list to develop a strategy for getting the chores done at their homes. Their solutions reflected the differences between their families.

Chores were a problem at Roxanne's house. No one ever seemed to remember to get them done. The problem was compounded by the fact that Roxanne's typical style for dealing with conflict was to **compromise.** Unfortunately every time she asked her two daughters, ages eight and eleven, to do something now, it turned into a bargaining session. She was tired of having to go through this. She decided to let the kids **problem-solve** a plan. At the same time she had to hold firm in her resolve not to be bargained out of whatever they agreed on. To stay out of this bargaining trap, Roxanne decided that they would write down their plan and have everyone sign it. She would make it clear to the kids that no changes could be made in the plan until they had a follow-up meeting the next weekend (**directing**).

The kids proposed that at the beginning of the month they would draw slips of paper from a jar and that the jobs would change once a month. Roxanne asked when she could expect the jobs to be done. They thought that right after school would be a good time. They all agreed that the kids could go out to play *after* the jobs were done ("**When you** _____, **then you can** _____.") The "contract" was written up and posted on the refrigerator. For the first part of the week the plan worked smoothly. Toward the end of the week, however, busy schedules kept them away from home in the afternoons, and chores were forgotten in the rush to get dinner on the table. When the family met to review the plan the next Saturday morning (**problem-solving**), everyone felt that the after-school chore time wasn't going to work. Their schedules were too erratic, and Roxanne was not always home right after school to see that the girls kept their agreement. Instead Saturday morning was chosen. They could do their chores all at once, and then do something fun together ("**When you** _____, **then you can** _____.") when they finished. The revised plan was posted, and it was a success.

Darrell, father of thirteen-year-old Lauren, also wanted to work on the chores issue. **Directing** was his style, and in the past he'd simply assigned his daughter tasks each week. Lauren was starting to balk at being ordered around by her dad. She'd stall around when it came time to do her jobs, and when she finally did them, they weren't done well. Darrell and Lauren were getting into regular verbal battles over this issue, and Darrell wanted solutions.

After some class discussion with parents of other teenagers, Darrell began to realize that at age thirteen Lauren probably needed to be making more decisions on her own. He decided to work with Lauren to come up with a plan.

In their **problem-solving** session Lauren said she was tired of doing chores such as emptying the trash and putting away laundry and that she wanted to cook dinners instead. This was news to Darrell, who had mistakenly assumed that Lauren was simply being rebellious. After some brainstorming Darrell **compromised** and agreed that Lauren would cook dinner two nights each week but that she would also be responsible for the cleanup, including loading the dishwasher and sweeping the kitchen floor. Part of the agreement was that dinner and cleanup would be done by seven o'clock, or the new agreement was off (**consequence**). After two weeks they would check in to see how the plan was going.

Understanding the limitations of their typical conflict style was a key for both Roxanne and Darrell in choosing strategies to create an effective plan of action for their families.

BEDTIME

Bedtime conflicts usually revolve around two problems: getting ready for bed and staying in bed once the lights are out. These are often interrelated. Let's look at two parents, both in the same class, who were having trouble with bedtime for very different reasons.

> Wes and Gretchen's six-year-old, Mindy, is an only child. They'd been having problems with bedtime since Mindy started school. Before that their schedule was flexible, and Mindy had often gone to bed when her parents did, which was past ten on most nights. Since she started grade school, however, waking her up in time for school made mornings miserable at their house. Because she was staying up late, she just wasn't getting enough sleep. Her teacher also reported that she seemed tired at school. In addition Wes and Gretchen were beginning to crave a little adult time in the evening. Gretchen was an **accommodator,** and Wes was an **avoider.** In fact he'd pretty much turned the parenting over to Gretchen. On the rare occasions when they joined forces to insist on Mindy's cooperation, Mindy would refuse altogether to get ready for bed, and her protests would set off a power struggle that left everyone upset and unsettled at bedtime. Wes and Gretchen were at their wits' end.

Here are some of the ideas from the list brainstormed by the class:

- Tell Mindy that if she is ready by eight o'clock, she and her parents can do a special activity together, such as reading a favorite book or playing a game of Mindy's choice.

- Establish a bedtime routine that starts earlier.

- Make a list of things that Mindy needs to do and post it where she can check off the items.

- A parent could get ready for bed early at the same time as Mindy and race with her to see who's done first. The winner gets to be read to, be given a shoulder rub, and so on.

- Have Mindy race a timer: See if she can be ready for bed (or school) before the timer rings.

- Problem-solve with her.

- If Mindy throws a tantrum, calmly tell her that you'll be ready to do an activity with her at eight-thirty if she's ready and then leave the room.

- If she's not ready by eight-thirty, she needs to go to bed earlier the next night.

Since Mindy was a power-struggle child (**underlying motive**), Wes and Gretchen decided that a plan would be more effective if she had some say in developing it. They chose to use **problem solving** with her. They realized that their avoiding-conflict styles had helped create the problem and that they would have to be clearer with Mindy that things needed to change at bedtime (**directing**). From the brainstormed list, both parents agreed that a regular bedtime routine would be helpful. They could enlist Mindy's help in planning the routine. Both Wes and Gretchen concurred that a need for attention might also be an **underlying motive.** When Mindy started school, Gretchen had taken a part-time job, and she was spending less time with her daughter than before. They planned to concentrate on using special one-on-one time with Mindy to address this need.

Wes and Gretchen sat down with Mindy and shared with her their frustration about bedtime (**feeling statements**). When they asked how she felt and used **attentive listening** to encourage her response, she admitted that she didn't like to go to bed feeling upset either. After brainstorming and evaluating (**problem solving**), they all agreed on a bedtime routine that would start at eight o'clock. Gretchen made a list of what needed to be done to get ready for bed, using little stick-figure pictures so that Mindy could read it. The list was posted on her bedroom door (**structure environment**). Each night Mindy would set the kitchen timer to see if she could be completely ready when the

timer went off at eight-thirty (**structure environment**).
They planned for fifteen minutes of card games after
that. If Mindy wasn't ready, she missed the card games
(**consequence**). If she wasn't sleepy when it was time
to go to bed, she could look at books quietly in her
bed (**compromise**).

The first few nights Mindy participated enthusiastically
in the plan. When she wasn't ready by eight-thirty one
night, she lost the card-playing privilege (**consequence**).
She got very angry and stomped to her room, slamming
the door and refusing to be tucked in. Wes and
Gretchen used **self-talk** to hang tough, reminding
themselves that this behavior was to be expected on the
heels of a new plan. The next night Mindy set the timer,
and the plan went off without a hitch. They had a
couple of rough nights after that, but generally bedtimes
got much easier.

The bedtime dilemma was a little different for Linda,
a single parent of three children. Her four-year-old,
Jacob, dragged his feet from the moment he started to
get ready for bed until the lights went out. Even then
he kept calling her back into his room, saying he was
afraid of the dark. Linda usually ended up lying down
with him until he fell asleep. On the one hand, Linda
was starting to feel resentful about how much time this
bedtime routine was taking. On the other hand, she
felt guilty about her resentful feelings because her
son's fears did seem real.

These are some of the ideas the class suggested once they heard
Linda's dilemma:

• Play story tapes or quiet music at bedtime to soothe Jacob.

• Set up a regular bedtime routine and stick to it.

• Provide a snuggly object, such as a special blanket or a favorite
stuffed animal.

• Give Jacob a soft object of Linda's to cuddle (bathrobe, etc.).

• Provide a night-light or other soft light in his room.

- Problem-solve with him.

- Sit in the doorway or just outside his room with a good book until he's asleep or for an agreed-upon amount of time. Reduce the time after a few nights. Agree that you will stay there as long as he is quiet. If he tries to talk to you, leave for five minutes.

- Find children's books on nighttime fears at your local library. Read these together and talk about them.

- Allow him to sleep on the floor of a sibling's room or move them into the same room.

- Be clear with him ahead of time about the bedtime plan.

- Plan special time together for one-on-one attention.

- Allow Jacob to read or look at books until he's ready to fall asleep.

- Each time he gets up, he owes time. He goes to bed five minutes earlier for each time he disturbs Linda after lights are out.

- Wake him up earlier in the morning so that it's easier for him to go to bed that night.

- Drop his daytime nap so that he'll be more ready for sleep.

> Linda decided that she would be uncomfortable with a solution that didn't acknowledge her son's very real fears, but she also needed to come up with a plan that would free up her time in the evening. She discussed the problem with Jacob (**feeling statement, attentive listening, and problem solving**), who couldn't identify anything specific that he was afraid of, except the dark. She suggested that they put a night-light in his room (**structure the environment**) and agreed to sit in the doorway (**compromise:** Linda gave up some time; Jacob gave up having his mother lie down with him). The morning that the plan went into effect, Linda reminded Jacob of the new policy. That night she read in his doorway as she had promised, and she was surprised at how smoothly the plan worked.

Most parents deal with bedtime struggles at some time in their parenting careers. The solutions vary with the family. Linda's son was struggling with his fear of the dark, which she addressed by devising a plan that fit her personality and values. Gretchen and Wes's daughter, Mindy's, bedtime trials involved a different approach, addressing attention and power motives. In Chapter 13, Ed and Nancy dealt with the same conflict in yet a different way. Each parent combined his or her creativity with the strategies they learned in our parenting classes to invent their own solution to this classic conflict.

GETTING READY IN THE MORNING

One of the ripest times for conflict is when the family is getting ready to leave the house in the morning. Each step in the process—from getting kids out of bed to getting them dressed, fed, and organized to leave—is a potential trouble spot.

> From the minute Kevin's feet hit the floor until he and his six-year-old son, Matt, were out the door, "Hurry up" was the constant refrain. Unfortunately, from his father's point of view, "Dawdle" was Matt's middle name, and he was driving his father crazy in the mornings. Ten minutes after telling his son it was time to get dressed, Kevin would find Matt sitting in front of his dresser trying to decide what to wear. A few minutes later his dad would find him still in pajamas, surrounded by the clothes he had selected, putting together a puzzle. As time got short, Kevin's reminders grew less and less gentle. Finally, in exasperation, Kevin would grit his teeth and stuff Matt into his clothes. Then Matt wouldn't be able to find his shoes. By the time they hit the car, Kevin was usually yelling at his son.

Kevin told our parenting class that consequences didn't seem to work with Matt. Kevin wasn't comfortable delivering him to school in his pajamas, but he did try putting him in the car, along with a bag stuffed with his clothes for the day. Matt was perfectly happy to get dressed in the car on the way to school. They even tried doing a special activity together if Matt could be ready before they needed to leave. It helped for a while, but most mornings they were just too rushed.

Other parents in the class grinned in recognition, having seen similar behavior in some of their own kids. This is a partial list of their ideas:

- Break getting dressed into specific tasks and have child check off each one on a list.
- Get dressed together.
- If he's not dressed, take him to school as he is and let him finish dressing there.
- Tell Matt that if he's ready on time, he can watch cartoons.
- Problem-solve together.
- Choose clothes the night before.
- Get up earlier.
- If Matt can't choose clothes in five minutes, then choose them for him.
- Put shoes in a specific place.
- Get dressed before breakfast, not after.
- Hand Matt his clothes to put on, piece by piece.
- Tell the teacher that Matt may be very late and take him to school when he's ready.
- Check with his teacher to see if there's a problem at school that makes Matt reluctant to go.
- Play "Beat the Clock" by racing a timer.

First Kevin realized that if he could stay calmer in the morning and get out of rush mode, it might help him to deal with his son more constructively. He planned to set his alarm fifteen minutes earlier to allow extra time. He would also use **self-talk** to stay relaxed. The next problem was figuring out how to get his son moving. Picking out clothes was definitely a trouble spot, so Kevin decided to have Matt do that before he went to bed the night before (**directing**). At a family meeting Kevin could bring up the problem of the shoes always being lost, and Matt and his older sister,

Petra, could help solve that one (**problem solving**). Since Matt seemed oblivious to whatever consequences Kevin tried, he thought the idea of getting dressed together might work, and might be fun too. Eventually he would move Matt toward getting dressed independently, but for now this might be a good solution.

At their next family meeting they worked on the lost-shoes issue. Matt agreed to locate his shoes before going to bed and to set them out with the rest of his clothes. If he forgot to do this and couldn't find them quickly, he could wear his rubber boots, which were always by the back porch (**consequence**).

At our next class session Kevin reported that the plan was going well. Matt especially liked getting dressed alongside his dad. He'd worn his rubber boots to school only once. Kevin was having a hard time getting himself up earlier, but the more relaxed mornings were a big incentive.

Frank was up against a different problem. His wife, Jamie, was one of those people who had everything highly organized, and she usually **directed** the family routines. Unfortunately when her job as a secretary in a local company went from part-time to full-time, she had to leave the house by seven, and the morning mission of getting everyone ready to go by eight fell to laid-back Frank (an **accommodator** and **avoider** until he blew his stack). Things didn't go so smoothly for Frank. In particular eleven-year-old Elissa was having trouble getting out of bed. Frank usually woke her at seven-fifteen, and from that time on he kept going back to her room to remind her to get up. Some mornings he got angry and literally threw the covers back and dragged her out of bed. Elissa often didn't get to the table until seven forty-five. After a quick breakfast she usually spent the next fifteen minutes rushing around to get out the door on time, leaving chaos in her wake.

Jamie and Frank both felt that if Elissa would get out of bed on time, the rest of the morning routine would flow more smoothly. They asked the class to help them brainstorm ideas:

- Put Elissa to bed earlier.

- Get Elissa an alarm clock.

- If she's not ready by the time the family leaves for school, she can walk to school.

- Tell Elissa that breakfast is cleared at seven forty-five. If she hasn't eaten, she can make her own.

- Start waking her up earlier.

- Trade time. (She owes Frank a job for the time it takes him to get her out of bed.)

- Problem-solve with her.

- Let her know that if she doesn't get up after the first call, you won't remind her again. Let her stay in bed and take the consequences for being late to school.

- Tickle her awake.

Frank and Jamie both agreed that Elissa needed to start taking responsibility for her own morning routines. They decided to buy a clock radio for her (**structure environment**) *and then let her get herself out of bed.*

At dinner one night Frank told Elissa how much it bothered him to be constantly reminding her to get going in the morning (**feeling statement**). When Frank suggested the clock-radio idea, Elissa was excited. They planned a father-daughter outing to purchase it and then go out to lunch together (**special time**). Elissa came home and set the clock radio so that she could wake up to her favorite rock station. Frank also asked if she thought she needed more sleep. Elissa said that she sometimes had a hard time falling asleep and asked for quiet reading time once she was in bed. Jamie and Frank agreed that as long as she seemed rested and could get herself moving in the morning, she could read quietly in her bed until nine-thirty and then turn out her own light (**compromise**).

Generally the plan worked well. Elissa occasionally missed the family breakfast, but most days she was ready to leave on time. And Frank was more than happy to give up his nagging role. The only catch was that they had to negotiate the volume of the rock music (sometimes **directing** with a **consequence** and sometimes **compromise**).

After they resolved the getting-out-of-bed issue, Jamie and Frank explored the bigger issue of Jamie letting go of her tight organization of the kids' lives (**parenting partnership**). They could see that Elissa had not learned Jamie's efficient organization by association and that she needed to take more responsibility for organizing her own time and possessions. Besides, with Jamie's more demanding work schedule, she just couldn't do it all anymore. Jamie and Frank came up with a list of responsibilities that could be turned over to the kids, such as room cleaning and packing lunches (**problem solving**). Jamie put some of her organizational energy into establishing regular family meetings, and together they problem-solved ways for family members to share responsibility for daily routines (**problem solving**).

SCREEN TIME

Technology has created a new set of concerns for parents. A common problem parents in our class encounter is out-of-control television and video use.

Vicki and Ken's fifteen-year-old son, Michael, was a bright child who had a natural love of games, so video games held great appeal for him. He saved his meager allowance for over a year to buy his first video-game system when he was twelve, and he continued to spend most of his disposable income on games. TV viewing was becoming a problem, too, since the video system included a television, and the whole setup was in his room. Vicki and Ken felt that Michael had a right to choose how he used it as long as his school grades didn't suffer. Lately, however, they had begun to notice that he was retreating to his room for longer periods of time and doing things with friends less and less. This bothered them both, and they brought their concern to the parenting class.

Although most of the members of our class were parents of younger children, many of them shared this concern about screen time. Here is a partial list of their brainstorms:

- Offer him a choice: Either he reduces his screen time or the video game/TV is put away for a specified amount of time.

- Throw the TV and game system away.

- Set a time limit for screen use.

- Make a policy that there will be no computer games during the week.

- Ground Michael if he plays computer games too much.

- Require Michael to spend a certain amount of time out of his room.

- Give him more jobs to do so that he doesn't have time to play.

- Let him play computer games only if he plays them with his parents.

- Move the game setup to a different room in the house.

- Find a hobby outdoors that his parents can share with Michael.

- Talk to him about the problem.

- Pay him one dollar for every day he stays away from the screen.

- Tell him he must get a job after school.

- Encourage him to go out for a sport.

- Ask him if he'd like to have some friends over.

- Take him to a therapist to figure out why he's withdrawing.

- Let him be. (It's typical of teenagers to hide out in their rooms.)

Ken and Vicki set aside time one evening to discuss the issue, and they used the list of suggestions as a starting point for **problem solving.** The discussion got a little heated over whether to encourage him to try out for sports because Vicki felt Ken's pushiness about sports had been damaging to Michael when he was younger. Ken agreed that Michael shouldn't be pressured to go out for a team, but insisted that he needed a physical outlet. He suggested that he and Michael take a tennis class together and play each other several times a week, since this would also meet Ken's own need for exercise.

Vicki reminded Ken about what they'd learned in their parenting class: Whenever possible, teens need to be involved in making decisions that concern them. They agreed to use the **problem solving** process with Michael on this issue.

Vicki and Ken decided that before meeting with Michael, the two of them would need to agree about what follow-through they might use if Michael didn't cooperate with the problem-solving approach. They agreed that they'd be willing to remove the machines from his room for a while (**consequence**) until they could reach agreement.

The next Saturday morning, when his little brother was at a friend's house, they sat down with Michael to discuss their concerns. Because they knew this was a touchy subject, they chose a time when they felt rested and prepared to use their best **listening and sharing skills.** Ken raised their concerns.

"We both feel like you're missing out on too much because you're spending time playing video games instead," Ken began. "We decided to discuss our concerns with you and see what we can work out together."

"Aw, c'mon. I don't see why you're so worried. I'm keeping up with my schoolwork, aren't I?" Michael retorted.

"So far your grades don't seem to have suffered, but we both feel you need to spend less time watching the screen and more time being involved with everyday life," Vicki calmly responded. "We feel so strongly about it that your dad and I will have to decide ourselves unless you help us out."

Michael knew from earlier problem-solving sessions that his suggestions would be taken seriously. He also knew that he might not like the decision his parents would make without his input.

"Okay. I'd rather have a say in it, I guess. I suppose I could agree not to play after ten o'clock," he offered.

After five minutes of brainstorming the three of them developed a plan: On school days Michael could play video games or watch TV until dinner, but in the evenings the machines would stay off. On weekends he could play for four hours, at times of his choosing. If he broke the agreement, he would lose the privilege of using the machine for a week.

As a part of the plan Ken and Vicki agreed to play some video games themselves so that they could better understand why Michael enjoyed them. Adding tennis lessons to the plan also appealed to Michael. This idea had the added bonus of giving them more time together. Both parents were surprised at how open Michael was to resolving the problem once his initial defensiveness and suspicion had worn off.

Ken and Vicki needed to put the system away only one time after the plan went into effect. They still bring up the issue now and then, and their joint solution has continued to evolve. Michael does have other interests now, and the video system is no longer the centerpiece of his life.

SIBLING TEASING

Despite its bad reputation with parents, sibling conflicts offer kids abundant opportunities to learn important social skills. They gain valuable experience setting boundaries and learning to respect others' privacy. Sibling rivals learn to share attention and (on the good days) to cooperate with others. They also learn to take teasing and put-downs, and to create verbal comebacks that are useful elsewhere. Much of this healthy learning is not easy on parents, however!

Many of us are confused about when to intervene and when to ignore teasing, bickering, and fighting. Sometimes kids enjoy engaging in low-key teasing and bickering, and no one is particularly bothered by it—except the parent of course. Many of these behaviors are bids for attention. When this is the case, **ignoring** may be the best strategy. If the disagreement is a small one, children may have sufficient skills to resolve the problem themselves. However, when sibling teasing and fighting results in injury or ongoing emotional or physical abuse, the parent must intervene. In a study on sibling violence psychologist Sandra Graham-Berman reported that one out of ten children experience physical abuse at the hands of their siblings. As adults half of these abused siblings remembered their parents as either not being aware of the problem or ignoring it.

One July in a parenting workshop sibling issues were a sizzling topic:

> By the middle of summer vacation Ellen was more than happy to send her two children, Andrea, age seven, and Sid, age eleven, to camp. What had promised to be a relaxing, enjoyable summer at home with the kids was quickly turning into a nightmare. Sid took every opportunity to mercilessly tease Andrea about everything, from her "baby" hairstyle to her toy pony collection. Andrea was developing her own coping strategies. When Sid pushed her to the boiling point, she would take a swing at her brother. One time she threw a punch that knocked a temporary cap off of Sid's front tooth. Sid wasn't the only one to initiate the troublesome behavior. Besides occasional random swipes, Andrea took delight in irritating Sid by grabbing him and kissing him. Of course Sid was repulsed by this, and he would immediately report the transgression to Ellen.

A murmur of empathy rippled through the room, and we knew that we were in for a good session. Several important ideas about sibling rivalry came out of our discussion:

- Help kids express their angry feelings toward their siblings in appropriate ways (with words, pictures, etc.).

- Keep your cool when your kids are going at it.

- Try not to lay blame. You never really know what little sister did to big brother before he whacked her.

- When one child assumes the victim role, it is important to work with both the victim and the aggressor to make behavior changes.

- Often negative sibling behavior is a bid for parental time and attention.

- Teasing may be a reflection of low self-esteem; the child may build himself up by putting down his sibling.

- Avoid comparing kids. Recognize each child as the unique individual he or she is.

- Be aware that your children's relationships with each other may reflect your relationship with your spouse.

After a general discussion of the issue, the group began brainstorming ways to combat Ken and Vicki's sibling problem:

- Send children outside to continue teasing and bickering: "You can bug each other if you want, but please go outside so I don't have to listen to it."

- Separate teasing/bickering/fighting siblings. Send both of them to their rooms or to different parts of the house with instructions to come out when they are ready to stop fighting.

- Sign kids up for more activities.

- Keep a "Things to Do When Bored" list on the refrigerator.

- Discuss the problem with the kids and work together to make a plan for change.

- Set up special time for each child.

- Send the child who is physically aggressive to his or her room.

- Ignore Andrea and Sid when they are teasing each other.

- A parent could take time out.

- Distract children into a fun activity.

- Plan a family celebration if children can reduce their bickering.

- Sit children in chairs facing each other. When they work out a solution to their problem, they can get out of the chairs.

As the story unfolded in our class, it became clear that these episodes occurred more frequently when either child was bored. Also, a need for attention might be contributing to the problem (**underlying motive**). Even though she had the summer off from her teaching job, Ellen was busy doing house projects and hadn't really spent much time with the children individually. She decided to **problem-solve** with the kids, bringing up boredom as part of the discussion. In the same meeting she would also set up a schedule for **special time** with each of her children.

At their next **family meeting** Ellen initiated the discussion: "Lately I've been really annoyed with all the teasing that's been going on between you two. It usually seems to end up with someone running to me because they're mad or hurt."

"But we like to do it. It's fun," replied Andrea.

"Well, it's not fun when someone gets mad or hurt, and it's not fun for me when I have to get involved," Ellen said. "Maybe we could think of a signal to give each other when it stops feeling like fun. I also noticed that the teasing happens more when one of you is bored. What do you two think about this problem?" After some discussion they brainstormed and developed a plan. They agreed to make a time-out hand signal to each other when the teasing started to heat up. They challenged themselves to come up with a list of thirty things to do when they were bored, and the finished product was posted on the bulletin board by the phone. Ellen also brought up the attention issue, and plans were made for regularly scheduled special time for the rest of the summer. In addition she informed the kids that from now on if one of them came running to her after a teasing bout, she was going to separate them by sending them to different parts of the house (**structure the environment**). Everyone liked the idea of checking back at their next family meeting and, if they were successful, celebrating by making banana splits together.

The rest of the summer was much calmer, though teasing was still a sport the children regularly enjoyed. When Ellen found it too annoying, she asked the kids to either stop or go outside (**offering choices**). Several times she used the separation idea. **Anger and cooling-off strategies** were also helpful when one of the kids blew up. With a few parenting tools in her pocket and a better understanding of the dynamics, Ellen stayed cooler and was more confident in her handling of this age-old conflict.

In addition to the strategies that the workshop participants brainstormed, you might also find it useful to refer to the "Guide to Helping Children Problem-Solve Together," Appendix A, in handling day-to-day sibling conflicts.

Many of the parenting resources currently available treat troublesome behaviors as if they were the same for all families. As we've seen by looking more closely at the five classic conflicts in this chapter, that isn't usually the case. Because of their willingness to bring the conflicts out into the open, each family was able to use the tools described in this book to invent a solution that met its own special needs.

16
The Journey

"A good traveler has no fixed plans and is not intent on arriving."

—*Lao-tzu*, Tao Te Ching

"The journey is home."

—*Nelle Morton, theologian*

THERE WAS ONCE A MAN WHO WAS A WANDERER. HE PASSED THE SAME house every year at spring, year after year. In this house there lived a man who had watched the traveler pass every spring.

"Why are you always going somewhere else?" he asked "Don't you ever long to stay put?"

The old wanderer replied, "It is true that I used to tire of traveling, but that is when I believed I was going somewhere else. I followed a map then, and I worried that I was on the wrong road. Now I know that each day brings a new path, and I trust that I will know the way when I am there. But now I am here, and while I am here, the journey is my home."

From the time we conceive our firstborn, we embark upon a journey of change. As much as we might like to stop the clock at this or that precious moment, we can't. So we might as well prepare to be at home on the road.

Lots of parenting programs offer a clear map and a fixed plan for the journey. Theirs is a comforting doctrine, listing concrete dos and don'ts that minimize parental uncertainty and claim universal practicality. They lull us into believing that children will pretty much grow up okay as long as we love them (or discipline them, or both) and follow a few simple rules. This reasoning has great appeal, since it saves us worry and self-doubt and it magnifies the powerful pull of our own upbringing in a more familiar, tradition-bound age. And this approach did work at an earlier time, when the world's rate of change was slower and kids were being prepared for more predictable lives.

The fixed map no longer works. Parents are unique individuals, and our plans need to reflect these differences. The children of the next century will need to be independent, critical, and creative thinkers if they are to solve problems that we haven't even begun to imagine. As members of a global community they will need to respect differences and to show concern and caring for all people.

It's our job to give them these tools for their journey into the future, but there is no clear map of the road, no doctrine that can teach us how to anticipate it. Yes, we do need to love them, and they do need structure and discipline. But we also must love them enough to give up our fixed plans and to prepare for the journey we take as families: the journey to practice the principles of peace, to bring our heartfelt ideals to our hearths. A peaceable family—one that is willing to allow conflict to surface so that it can be resolved, where self-esteem is nurtured, where members feel safe and respected and are taught caring and concern for others—provides us with the setting to give children these tools.

The examples, suggestions, and tips we offer here are not meant to be used as a fixed plan for the road. Instead we're offering you tools for creating your own fluid plans and a basic framework for nurturing your own unique children.

It's up to you to listen to your children, to come to know them, to listen to yourself and come to trust yourself more, to develop your parenting intuition. Many of the ideas in the book will help you do that. By trying them out you'll become more and more clear about what works for you and your kids in your own special lives. You'll be prepared to create your own process for making peace at home, not without conflict but with your own individual way of dealing with it.

We're still on the journey, along with lots of other parents. Join us on the journey home.

If you would like to know more about our workshops for parents or teachers, write us at:

460 S.W. Madison, #12
Corvallis, OR 97333

A Guide to Helping Children Solve Problems Together

As with any other new skill, children may need some help in getting started using problem solving themselves. Your primary job is to help maintain focus on the problem and on the process of problem solving. Stay neutral, and keep your role as minimal as possible.

IS COOLING OFF NEEDED BEFORE BEGINNING?

Ask for agreement on basic ground rules:

• **Avoid blaming, interrupting, or name-calling.**

• **Work together to solve the problem.**

1. **Gather information.**
   Give each child a chance to tell what happened and how they are feeling.
   Encourage them to use feeling statements and attentive listening:

   "What happened?"
   "How did you feel when _____?"

2. State the problem so that it expresses everyone's needs.

"You want _____, and you want _____. What can you do so that everyone will be happy?" or *"What can you do to help meet everyone's needs?"*

3. Encourage the children to generate ideas.
Accept all ideas, both crazy and practical, without criticism.

"Let's see how many ideas we can think of to solve this problem."
"Remember, anything goes, no matter how crazy, and we don't criticize any ideas when we're brainstorming."

Write down all ideas.
You may need to remind kids what the problem is by restating it frequently:

"Remember, the problem we're working on is _____."

4. Evaluate.
Look at the consequences of each idea.

"What might happen if you [state idea]?"
"Is that something that would make both people happy?"
"How can we work toward meeting everyone's needs?"

5. Make a plan.

Ask the children for a solution and help them carry it out if necessary.
Evaluate the decision later together and decide together if it worked.

If the plan wasn't successful, plan for more problem solving when appropriate.
If the plan was successful, congratulate them on their problem-solving abilities.

Action Plan for Change: A Guide to Tackling Troublesome Behaviors

MAKE A PLAN:

1. Choose what you would like to change. Ask yourself, *What would save my energy the most?*

2. Does the unacceptable behavior reflect some unmet need of your child? If so, address this need in the plan, as well as strategies for changing the behavior. Don't let this prevent you from taking action for change.

3. State to yourself what behavior will change and how it will change.

4. Brainstorm ideas. Think creatively.

5. Evaluate ideas and formulate a plan, using these questions to guide you:

Which ideas are age appropriate and workable, given the temperament of your child?

Which ideas will balance your typical conflict-resolution style?

Which ideas are practical, given your schedule and lifestyle?

What are you willing to do, based on your personal values and beliefs?

Also, plan a follow-through strategy, such as what consequences to use if kids don't cooperate *or* plan to problem-solve the issue in a family council. If you decide to bring it to a family meeting, think ahead about which aspects, if any, are nonnegotiable.

IMPLEMENT YOUR PLAN:

1. Discuss the issue with your child or your family.

"We've been making some mistakes. We are going to start doing things differently."

State the problem clearly and how it makes you feel.
"I get really frustrated when I call the family to dinner and you don't respond. I'm hungry by the time I get dinner on the table and I want to sit down and eat while it's still hot."

Problem-solve with the family (see Chapter 10).
Optional: Have family decide on consequences. Ask:
"What should I do if you don't _____?"

Write down the plan and post it.
Plan a fun family activity.

2. Give kids one reminder. At breakfast say:

"Tonight is the first night to try our new plan for coming to dinner when I call you. Everyone remember what we talked about?"

3. Be firm and clear. If your resolve starts to weaken, get support from your partner and/or remind yourself of the importance of what you are teaching your children in holding firm. *They have to learn to be considerate of the needs of other people in the family. They also need to get the message that when I ask them to do something, I mean it.*

4. Be respectful. How you say it is as important as what you say. Avoid blaming, name-calling, and sarcasm.

5. Cool off if necessary before following through.

6. Follow through. Demonstrate to your children that you are serious by following through if they don't respond: If they don't come to the table within three minutes of being called, clear their plate from the table and get on with dinner. (Inform them ahead of time that this is the consequence so that they know what to expect if they choose not to come.) If in doubt about how to follow through when you're on the spot, buy time by saying, *"I need to cool off. I'll let you know what the consequences are later."*

Hints:

- **Make the change a priority in your life.** Think about your plan at different times during the day and mentally rehearse what you will do. When it is time to act on it, give it your full attention. Be prepared to set aside what you are doing to deliver a consequence if necessary.

- **Expect the kids to resist the change at first.** Hold firm!

- **Change takes time.** You may need to remind yourself of this frequently.

- **Special time and playful family activities will facilitate change.**

- **Nurture yourself.** Usually the process of bringing about a change is stressful. It will take extra energy and time on your part to hold firm to your plan and to respond to your child's resistance. Go out to a movie, take a walk, or plant some new flowers in your garden.

- **Plan ahead what self-talk you will use to avoid sabotaging your own efforts by falling into old, disabling patterns.**

Appendix C

Peacing It Together: The Tools

Use this chart as an all-in-one reference guide as you make your plan of action for dealing with conflicts. The five categories list various tools that can help.

SETTING LIMITS	CLIMATE BUILDING	FAMILY STRUCTURE	PARENT EMPOWERMENT
C.H.O.I.C.E.S. *Command (p.96)* *Humor or Surprise (p.109)* *Offer Choices (p.98)* *Ignore (p.107)* *Compromise (p.102)* *Encourage Problem Solving (p.115)* *Structure the Environment (p.112)* Follow-through: *Direct Action (p.66)* *"When you ——, then you can ——." (p.66)* *Consequences (p.67)*	*Special Time (p.166)* *Attentive Listening (p.125)* *Feeling Statements (p.127)* *Adult Anger and Cooling-Off Strategies (p.37)* *Kids' Anger and Cooling-Off Strategies (p.136)* *Cooperative Activities (p.170)* *Family Identity (p.171)* *Humor (p.172)*	*Family Meetings (p.146)* *Parenting-Partnership Meetings (p.157)*	*Self-talk for Self-defeating Messages (p.62)* *Adult Anger and Cooling-Off Strategies (p.37)* *Self-nurturing (p.174)* *Attentive Listening (p.125)* *Feeling Statements (p.127)*
			CHILD EMPOWERMENT
			Kids' Anger and Cooling-Off Strategies (p.136) *Problem Solving (p.115)* *Family Meetings (p.146)* *Guide to Helping Children Problem-Solve Together (p.201)* *Attentive Listening (p.125)* *Feeling Statements (p.127)*

Bibliography and Suggested Resources

*Indicates books and materials that parents in our classes have found especially helpful.

Albert, Linda. *A Teacher's Guide to Cooperative Discipline.* Circle Pines, Minn.: American Guidance Service, 1989.

Ames, Louise Bates. *Your One-Year-Old: The Fun-loving, Fussy Twelve- to Fourteen-Month Old.* New York: Dell Publishing, 1983.

———. *Your Two-Year-Old: Terrible or Tender.* New York: Dell Publishing, 1980.

Ames, Louise Bates, and Carol Chase Haber. *Your Eight-Year-Old: Lively and Outgoing.* New York: Delacorte Press, 1989.

———. *Your Nine-Year-Old: Thoughtful and Mysterious.* New York: Dell Publishing, 1987.

———. *Your Seven-Year-Old: Life in a Minor Key.* New York: Dell Publishing, 1985.

Ames, Louise Bates, and Francis L. Ilg. *Your Five-Year-Old: Sunny and Sincere.* New York: Dell Publishing, 1979.

———. *Your Four-Year-Old: Wild and Wonderful.* New York: Dell Publishing, 1976.

———. *Your Six-Year-Old: Loving and Defiant.* New York: Dell Publishing, 1979.

———. *Your Three-Year-Old: Friend or Enemy.* New York: Dell Publishing, 1976.

Ames, Louise Bates, Frances L. Ilg, and Sidney M. Baker. *Your Ten-to Fourteen Year-Old.* New York: Dell Publishing, 1988.

Brazelton, T. Berry. *Families: Crisis and Caring.* Reading, Mass.: Addison-Wesley Publishing Co., 1989.

*Brusko, Marlene. *Living with Your Teenager.* New York: Ballantine Books, 1986.

*Cline, Foster, and Jim Fay. *Parenting with Love and Logic.* Colorado Springs, Colo.: NavPress, 1990.

*Coloroso, Barbara. *Winning at Parenting . . . Without Beating Your Kids.* Videotape. Littleton, Colo.: Kids Are Worth It!, 1989.

*Crary, Elizabeth. *Kids Can Cooperate.* Seattle: Parenting Press, 1984.

*_____. *Pick Up Your Socks . . . And Other Skills Growing Children Need!* Seattle: Parenting Press, 1990.

Clarke, Jean Illsley. *Self Esteem: A Family Affair.* Minneapolis: Winston Press, 1978.

Clarke, Jean Illsley, and Connie Dawson. *Growing Up Again: Parenting Ourselves, Parenting Our Children.* New York: HarperCollins Publishers, 1989.

Community Board Program, Inc. *Classroom Conflict Resolution Training for Elementary Schools.* San Francisco, Calif.: The Community Board Program, Inc., 1987.

Crum, Thomas. *The Magic of Conflict.* New York: Simon and Schuster, Inc., 1987.

*Curran, Dolores. *Stress and the Healthy Family.* San Francisco: Harper & Row, 1985.

_____. *Traits of a Healthy Family.* New York: Ballantine Books, 1983.

Deacove, Jim. *Cooperative Games Manual.* Perth, Canada: Family Pastimes, 1974.

Dunn, Corey, and Janet Mann, comp. *The Family Council.* Albany, Oreg.: Linn-Benton Educational Service District.

Eyre, Linda and Richard. *Teaching Children Responsibility.* New York: Ballantine Books, 1984.

*Faber, Adele, and Elaine Mazlish. *How to Talk So Kids Will Listen & Listen So Kids Will Talk.* New York: Avon Books, 1980.

*_____. *Siblings Without Rivalry.* New York: Avon Books, 1987.

Fay, Jim. *Helicopters, Drill Sergeants and Consultants.* Audiotape. Golden, Colo.: Cline/Fay Institute, Inc. 1986.

Fay, Jim, and Foster Cline. *Setting Limits for Kids.* Audiotape. Golden, Colo.: Cline/Fay Institute, Inc. 1986.

Fisher, Roger, and William Ury. *Getting Together: Building a Relationship That Gets to Yes.* Boston: Houghton Mifflin Co., 1988.

_____. *Getting to Yes.* Boston: Houghton Mifflin Co., 1981.

Fluggleman, Andrew. *The New Games Book*. Garden City, N.Y.: Dolphin Books/Doubleday and Co., 1976.

Gilbert, Jerrold. "Logical Consequences: A New Classification." *Journal of Individual Psychology* 42 (no. 2): 243.

Glenn, H. Stephen. *Developing Capable People*. Audiotapes. (Available as part of the Developing Capable People Seminars.) Provo, Utah: Sunrise Press, 1989.

*———. *Developing Healthy Self-Esteem*. Videotape. Fair Oaks, Calif.: Sunrise Productions, 1989.

Glenn, H. Stephen, and Jane Nelsen. *Raising Self-Reliant Children in a Self-Indulgent World*. Rocklin, Calif.: Prima Publishing and Communications, 1989.

Gordon, Thomas. *Parent Effectiveness Training*. New York: Peter H. Wyden, Inc., 1970.

Israeloff, Roberta. "Mad Doesn't Mean Bad." *Working Mother*. February 1990.

Kreidler, William J. *Creative Conflict Resolution: More Than 200 Activities for Keeping Peace in the Classroom*. Glenview, Ill.: Scott Foresman, 1984.

Lerner, Harriet G. *The Dance of Anger*. New York: HarperCollins, 1989.

LeShan, Eda. *When Your Child Drives You Crazy*. New York: St. Martin's Press, 1985.

Lieberman, Susan A. *New Traditions: Redefining Celebrations for Today's Family*. New York: Farrar, Strauss and Giroux, 1991.

Luvmour, Saambhava and Josette. *Everyone Wins! Cooperative Games and Activities*. Philadelphia, Pa.: New Society, 1990.

McGinnis, Kathleen and James. *Parenting for Peace and Justice*. Maryknoll, N.Y.: Orbis Books, 1983.

———. *Parenting for Peace and Justice, Ten Years Later*. Maryknoll, N.Y.: Orbis Books, 1990.

Miller, Alice. *For Your Own Good*. New York: Farrar, Straus and Giroux, 1984.

Morton, Nelle. *The Journey Is Home*. Boston: Beacon Press, 1985.

*Nelsen, Jane. *Positive Discipline*. New York: Ballantine, 1987.

*Nelsen, Jane, and Lynn Lott. *I'm on Your Side: Resolving Conflict With Your Teenage Son or Daughter*. Rocklin, Calif.: Prima Publishing and Communications, 1990.

Orlick, Terry. *The Cooperative Game and Sports Book*. New York: Pantheon Books, 1978.

Osborne, Peter. *Parenting for the Nineties*. Intercourse, Pa.: Good Books, 1990.

Palo Alto Medical Foundation. LifeSkills Project. 400 Channing Ave., Palo Alto, Calif. 94301.

Popkin, Michael H., Edward J. Garcia, and Harry Woodward. *Active Parenting Discussion Program, Parent's Handbook.* Atlanta, Ga.: Active Parenting, Inc., 1983. (Available as part of the Active Parenting classes, which are offered in many communities.)

Rubin, Dr. Jeffrey, and Dr. Carol Rubin. *When Families Fight.* New York: William Morrow and Co., 1989.

Rubin, Nancy. "Mom's Style, Dad's Style." *Parents.* July 1988.

*Schmidt, Fran, and Alice Friedman. *Fighting Fair for Families.* Miami Beach, Fla.: Grace Contrino Abrams Peace Education Foundation, Inc., 1989.

Slagle, Robert. *A Family Meeting Handbook: Achieving Family Harmony Happily.* Sebastopol, Calif.: Family Relations Foundation, 1985.

Tannen, Deborah. *You Just Don't Understand.* New York: Ballantine Books, 1990.

Tavris, Carol. *Anger, the Misunderstood Emotion.* New York: Simon and Schuster, 1989.

Taylor, John. *Anger Control Training for Children and Teens.* Doylestown, Pa.: mar*co products, inc., 1991.

_____. "Parent Education: How to Do It," and "Creative, Corrective, and Therapeutic Answers to Children's Misbehavior," Spring 1987. Seminars Unlimited Northwest, Salem, Oreg. Seminar.

Ury, William. *Getting Past No: Negotiating with Difficult People.* New York: Bantam Books, 1991.

These companies make and sell a variety of cooperative board games:

Family Pastimes, RR4 Perth, Ontario, Canada, K7H3C6.
Animal Town, P.O. Box 485, Healdsburg, Calif. 95448

Index